CARAVAGGIO

His Incongruity & His Fame

BERNARD BERENSON

CARAVAGGIO

HIS INCONGRUITY
AND HIS FAME

1953

CHAPMAN & HALL
LONDON

Printed in Great Britain by Butler & Tanner Ltd., Frome and London
CAT. NO. 4168/4

TO THE MEMORY OF

ALDO DE RINALDIS

καλοῦ κἀγαθοῦ

ACKNOWLEDGEMENTS

ALINARI : 5, 11, 13, 14, 28, 30, 31, 32, 34, 46, 47, 51, 56, 64, 76

ANDERSON : 1, 4, 7, 12, 19, 20, 21, 22, 23, 27, 40, 48, 55, 60, 62, 73, 74, 86

BRENWASSER : 78

BROGI : 52

BULLOZ : 25

CHRIST CHURCH LIBRARY, OXFORD : 15

STEPHEN CLARKE, NEW YORK : 37

COURTAULD INSTITUTE, LONDON : 9

A. DINGJAN, THE HAGUE : 84

U. FINI, TREVISO : 72

FOGG MUSEUM, CAMBRIDGE, MASS. : 16

FOTOTECA BERENSON : 17, 33, 53, 59, 61, 77, 83

GABINETTO FOTOGRAFICO NAZIONALE : 41, 82

HANFSTAENGL : 10, 49, 50, 57, 58, 65, 75

IMPERIAL, MESSINA : 71

ISTITUTO CENTRALE DEL RESTAURO : 24, 70

MURRAY K. KEYES, NEW YORK : 2

V. KORDA, LONDON : 8

DENIS MAHON COLLECTION, LONDON : 80

MUSEUM OF ART, KANSAS CITY : 54

MUSEUM OF FINE ARTS, BOSTON : 3

MUSEUM OF MODERN ART, NEW YORK : 43

NATIONAL GALLERY, LONDON : 36, 38, 39

NATIONAL GALLERY, MELBOURNE : 79
ROBERT TREAT PAINE, JNR., CAMBRIDGE, MASS. : 6
MARIO PEROTTI, MILANO : 45
RHEIN. MUSEUM, COLOGNE : 85
ROHONCZ COLLECTION : 18
GUSTAVO SCHWARZ, BERLIN : 26, 44
SOPRINTENDENZA MONUMENTI, MILANO : 35
SOPRINTENDENZA MONUMENTI, NAPOLI : 66, 67
SOPRINTENDENZA MONUMENTI, PERUGIA : 88
SOPRINTENDENZA UFFIZI, FIRENZE : 29, 42
STATE MUSEUM OF BAVARIA : 87
STATE MUSEUM, COPENHAGEN : 81
LA VALLETTA MUSEUM : 68, 69
WADSWORTH ATHENEUM, HARTFORD, CONN. : 63

INTRODUCTION

This essay is to be about Caravaggio.[1]

Until now, either because I had no leisure or because my curiosity was not sufficiently roused, or perhaps for both these reasons, I have put off trying to get on intimate terms with Caravaggio. It happens in life that one hears of this or that person who fascinates one's friends but remains outside one's own private circle, even if we have met again and again. Then a happy accident dissipates the opaque film that kept one from seeing the whole of the hitherto fragmentary

[1] I am grateful to Professor Roberto Longhi for his brave effort to establish the canon of Caravaggio's works, autograph and copies. Zahn's *Caravaggio* (Berlin, Albertus Verlag, 1928) has been helpful and I have profited by all of Lionello Venturi's essays on Caravaggio and by the following works : Rouchés, *Le Caravage* (Paris, Alcan, 1900) ; M. Marangoni, *Il Caravaggio* (Firenze, L. Battistelli, 1922) and *Arte Barocca* (Firenze, Vallecchi, 1927) ; M. L. Patrizi, *Il Caravaggio* (Rinaldo Simboli, Recanati, 1921) ; Hermann Voss, *Die Malerei der Spätrenaissance in Rom und Florenz* (Berlin, G. Grotesche Verlag, 1920) ; Giuliano Briganti, *Il Manierismo Pellegrino Tibaldi* (Roma, Cosmopolita, 1945) ; Denis Mahon, *Studies in Seicento Art and Theory* (London, the Warburg Institute, 1937) ; Aldo de Rinaldis, *Neapolitan Painting of the Seicento* (Pantheon, Firenze) ; R. Longhi, *Mostra del Caravaggio e dei Caravaggeschi* (Milano : Aprile/Giugno 1951 ; Firenze, Sansoni).

acquaintance and one grows zestful to come close to him and to know him in his entirety.

I shall begin by looking at his, Caravaggio's, extant works.

Until a few decades ago his artistic personality was as nebulous as Leonardo's or Giorgione's before Giovanni Morelli. Almost any canvas was attributed to him that was startlingly lit, that represented figures with plumed hats, vulgar obese giants blasphemously posing as Christ and His disciples, dice-throwing or card-sharping undermen, jumbles of over-jolly, swilling, embracing males and females, or more decorous musical parties.

It is different now. Caravaggio has ceased to be a class or kind and has become as much of an artistic personality as Leonardo, or Giorgione at least.

I shall study those paintings only which are beyond any reasonable question his, and so recognized by students whose judgement we value. About those pictures I shall allow myself to say anything that comes into my head, a head that for many years has been meditating over art matters aesthetically, historically, ethically. In conclusion, I may allow myself to say a number of things that the examination of Caravaggio's work has suggested.

PART ONE

I

Proceeding somewhat chronologically, we shall look first at the basket of grapes, apples and figs with their foliage now at the Ambrosiana in Milan (Plate 1). Amber, honey, purple, green, brown, rose, distinct yet singing together, pearly grapes, figs bursting with succulence, bulging apples, leafage still erect, fresh, or on the other hand drying and dropping, but all with contours as precise as jewels. Elegance of every stalk, every vein, every twig.

Note that there is but faint indication of a ledge for the basket to rest on, and no suggestion of space, not even of a void, hardly more than in Chinese flower-painting.

In the Kress Collection there is a canvas representing pears, apples, grapes, scarcely any flowers and a glass jar half filled with water (Plate 2). This time they rest on a table covered with a cloth and the background is dark. No thought of space.

A painting of poppies rising proudly out of a wineflask may be seen in the Boston Museum of Fine Arts (Plate 3). The flask is wound round by ropes, and serpent-like coils of rope seem to wriggle out of the canvas. From the mouth of the globular flask riot grape-leaves—the whole on a ledge of some kind. No indication of space.

In Western art from the XIVth century on, flowers rioted over the illuminated vellum and adorned many an altarpiece by Gentile da Fabriano and Angelico. Fruits attracted sculptors first, and Donatello brought them to Padua, where Mantegna, Tura, Crivelli and their fellow-painters gathered them to garland their pictures with. Their flowers more often than not sprang out of vases, or cruses, or bottles, or pots. And everywhere silk hangings, drifted perhaps from far-away China, followed later by Turkey carpets. So many pretexts for the painting of what is now called " still-life ". Technique had sufficiently advanced to permit the artist to satisfy his itch to paint what interested him, regardless of symbolical or ethical meaning. Yet nobody thought or dared to make pictures of them in and for themselves, and not merely as ornaments or accessories to sacred subjects. In the North it may have been earlier perhaps, but in Italy still-life came late to a career of its own, later than the first to escape, the portrait, and later even than landscape, which till the XIXth century scarcely ever appears without some faint pretence at a story.

We find nearly the same basket of fruit and foliage in two other early works. In the young Fruit-seller of the Borghese Gallery it is almost identical. In the Uffizi Bacchus it is more varied and garlands the head.

The " Fruit-seller " (Plate 4) is a languishing youth in a situation unsuited to his temperament, for he is the kind of youth who when mature easily becomes an agitator. He holds the basket against his chest and cries the fruit with less interest in them than in himself. Plastic, crystalline shoulders and hands as over-modelled as Rubens at times.

What a contrast with the Bacchus ! (Plate 5). As a figure almost more Eastern than Italian, closer to Indo-Chinese sculpture, from the Graeco-Buddhic period down to our XVIIIth century and later, and found everywhere from Karachi to Osaka.

Why not ? Did not Bacchus come from India ? He corresponds startlingly to the visual image I had of the Bacchus of Euripides as

interpreted by Verral, or strangely enough to
the presentation of the god by Ninchi in the
same play, given forty years ago in the Roman
theatre at Fiesole. As fleshly as Antinous but
debonair, easily amused, a boon companion.
Yet do not presume : you may not be his play-
fellow but only his plaything. Ambivalent, he
meditates. Is it over the wine in the goblet, or
what merry sport it will be to intoxicate and to
hypnotize the ecstatic host of his followers till
they tear each other limb from limb ? He is an
Indian god, destroyer no less than preserver.

What could have been in the artist's mind when
he painted this image ? Perhaps only how to
draw it, how to pose it, how to paint it, the rest
an unearned increment. As contour, the en-
veloping curves of naked shoulder and arm are
out-and-out Manet.

It is just conceivable, although highly improbable, that a Far Eastern fly-leaf fell under
Caravaggio's eyes and subconsciously inspired
imitation. If a tall early Chinese bronze vase
could reach ancient Rome [1] and an Indian
ivory statuette of considerable dimensions and

[1] See Birgit Vessberg, " Un bronze du style Hoccai
découvert à Rome " (*Bulletin of the Museum of Far-Eastern
Antiquities*, Stockholm, No. 9, pp. 127–31).

bulk could reach provincial Pompei in Antiquity,[1] it surely was as easy, through Catholic missionaries of every order, or through Portuguese and Dutch traders, for a print to reach Rome at the end of the XVIth century, then, as never again since Antiquity, the capital of Europe. One such woodcut is a block print of the Kamakura period dated 1242, belonging to Mr. Robert T. Paine of Boston, here reproduced (Plate 6).

Similar still-life elements, fruit, leafage and a similar half-nude, are the constituent elements of an ivy-crowned youth in the Borghese Gallery, this time with a bunch of grapes in his right hand (Plate 7). He is more proletarian even than the boy bitten by a lizard (of whom presently), slightly negroid, wistful in an animal way. Professor Longhi calls him " the sick Bacchus ". If so, it leads one to fancy that some such concept may have haunted Caravaggio as was realized by Walter Pater in his Dionysiac " Denis de l'Auxerrois ". Here too I cannot resist declaring my admiration of a nude arm and shoulder that Manet might have painted if he had imitated Ingres.

[1] See Amedeo Maiuri, " Statuetta eburnea di Arte Indiana a Pompei " (*Le Arte*, I, 1938–9, pp. 111–15).

Fruit and flowers and leafage take part in yet another early painting formerly at Nuneham Park and now in the collection of Mr. Vincent Korda of London (Plate 8). A lizard darts out of their midst and bites a boy who starts back as much with disgust as with pain. What the special relations are between foreground and background is not clear, although a diagonal at the top may indicate a ceiling, and therefore an interior with a light from left to right—a predilection which grew on Caravaggio with the years. The chief interest (for me at least) is in the action and expression. The last particularly is something relatively new in Italian art, which before Caravaggio tended to be either existential, as is generally the case, or heroically, nobly expressive. A look of loathing as in this painting must have struck contemporaries as a startling innovation.

It is tempting to go on with the examination of other young men or boys posing as the Baptist, or as David, or Narcissus, whom Caravaggio seems to have enjoyed painting through his Roman years. I shall put it off to a more appropriate moment, and continue our study in a chronological order.

Since the above paragraphs were written,

Mr. David Carritt has discovered in the collection of Lieut.-Commander J. Thwaites a " Concert " (now in the Metropolitan Museum in New York), which Mr. Denis Mahon has published in the *Burlington Magazine* for January 1952 (Plate 9). A handsome youth listlessly strums a lute with his right hand, while his left fingers the keys. He is open-mouthed as if humming. To the right, a barebacked youth facing the other, but intent on a partition. To the left, above the voluminous folds of the luteplayer's mantle, appears a naked boy, who stoops to tie grapes in bunches.

Here are all the elements we have met already while looking at Caravaggio's earlier works. The same youngsters, the same mood of disdain, fatigue, melancholy as in some of them, the same bunches of grapes, the same unusual instruments, the same ignoring of space. The difference, if any, is that this composition is more frankly an " academy ", a studio arrangement of bare backs and of elaborate draperies. As in so much of " classical " art, the figures exist and make us enjoy their existence. They tell no story—none that my kind of picture-lover can hear.

Again flowers and fruit, and yet another and earlier predilection of still-life painters, namely, musical instruments, attract attention as we

C.—B

enjoy the most charming of all the Caravaggios that have come down to us. It is a young Roman girl playing the lute, now in the Hermitage (Plate 10). She sits by a table, and as she plays she looks far away and hums to herself. The space relations resemble the last, but while the foreground is more realized, the rest is left dubious.

Musical instruments attracted painters early, and they appear so often in XIVth-century altarpieces that special books have been written on the subject, and a great scholar, Julius Schlosser, gave them serious study. Musical instruments satisfy the painter's itch to represent with precision shapes that are in themselves geometrical. It may be one of the reasons why artists, the Protestant Dutch, for instance, took to painting concerts when they were no longer ordered to execute altarpieces.

The contrast between this luteplayer we have been enjoying and the figure I shall speak of now (Doria Gallery, Plate 13) is as between happiness and despair. This time it is a young woman with her head falling over her breast, sitting crushed and abandoned in an attitude of lonely misery. As with closed eyes and folded hands she nurses her grief, she knows that for her there is little sympathy and still less under-standing. (How different from the lyrically expressive treatment by Botticelli of a creature shut out of her world !) (Plate 12).

It is not easy to understand where she sits and how she is lit. It would seem in a dismal cell, dark except for a wedge of light in the upper right-hand corner.

Her dress of a stuff woven with a large pattern of dismembered flower and leaf has a skirt resting on the ground so stiff that its ornaments are as unmodelled as if on a wallpaper.

Nothing to indicate that she represents the penitent Magdalen except the exquisitely painted oil-flask.

The same model comes with little change into another Doria picture, "The Rest in the Flight" (Plate 11). Here it serves for the Madonna who is fast asleep, with her head bent over the Child also sound asleep. This to our right. To our left, a unique episode, and one would like to know if it was Caravaggio himself who had the idea, or if it was dictated to him by others, poets, men of letters.

A slim, dainty creature with half-folded wings, nude except for a drapery swirling around waist and seat, stands with back turned to us, but with

face in profile to left. He plays on a viol the
air on the partition held out with both hands by
Joseph who sits on his luggage. Between them
appears the head of a donkey. All this under a
spreading oak, with lush leafage and foliage on
the ground and a marshy woodland distance.
Truly a Shakespearian idyll painted by a
romantic artist nearer to Tintoretto than to Titian
and halfway between the latter and Poussin, but
so much gayer and sunnier than the so-serious
Frenchman. Even as composition, with the
figures invaded as it were by the landscape, it is
redolent of the art of Veronese and Tintoretto.
Only the angel in proportions and contour may
point to contact with the works of Correggio.

II

We now approach a phase in Caravaggio's
career when Giorgionesque features appear not
only in the treatment of light and shade but in
the placing of the figures and in their picturesque
romantic clothing, striped jerkins and plumed

hats and bonnets. Almost they remind us of the extravagances of the XVIIth-century imitator of Giorgione, Pietro Muttoni della Vecchia (1605–78).

The earliest and most attractive work of this phase is the " Soldier and Gypsy " in the Louvre (Plate 14). It is a picture I have loved for more than sixty years and never fail to renew acquaintance with when in Paris, and always with joy.

So quizzical as she touches his palm while sizing up the self-satisfied gullibility of the young peacock in his brand-new outfit with gloved hand on hip roguishly appraising her ; and neither she nor he is unaware of what may happen after the fortune-telling.

How different from another picture to which a Venetian critic almost contemporary with Giorgione gave the same title, I mean that artist's so-chaste, so-severe, so-lyrical " Soldier and Gipsy " now in the Venice Academy.

The placing of the two figures is Giorgionesque, and so is the tension as of a perpetual inner vibration unrelated to the momentary action and expression.

Nor can I refrain from mentioning the colour. It is curiously precious and savoury, and my eye enjoys it as my palate enjoys an exquisitely satisfying liqueur. I know few paintings which affect me the same way.

More obviously Giorgionesque is a composition in the Christ Church Library, Oxford, identified by Professor Longhi as Caravaggio's, although existing in copies only (Plate 15). A young woman, finishing her toilet, lays her left hand on a large round mirror, while the right hand holds a flower against her breast. She turns towards another young woman in profile who argues eagerly with her—Martha reproving Mary. She reminds one of many a Venetian figure by Palma, by Bonifazio, by Titian, by Lotto.

Giorgionesque again is the innocent boy in the picture of youths playing cards now in the Fogg Museum, Cambridge, Mass. (Plate 16). His head, as shape, as form, as lighting, reminds one of the youngest of the three half-lengths in the Pitti Gallery still labelled Lotto but by a greater master in whom Bellini and Giorgione meet.

This may well be one of the earliest of Caravaggio's picaresque paintings. Few artists have depicted concentration more convincingly : the younger boy so intent on the cards, and the others watching for the instant to cheat him. As action dramatic to a degree, as drawing, as modelling, as lighting, it is a masterly achievement, rivalling the best that Velasquez did in his early years, the Velasquez who was not only the greatest but in many ways the closest of Caravaggio's followers.

A more developed treatment of the same subject used to be in the Sciarra Collection in Rome, a typical Venetian " three-figure " picture (Plate 17). Vibrating with eagerness are two of them, all the more strung up because of the deep concentration of the charming youth whom the two first are leaping to swindle.

As composition, as action, it is a masterpiece, somewhat spoiled for me by the too-dramatized contrast between vice and virtue ; by the too villainous head of the older, the central, figure.

Yet these seem to have been the elements that fascinated Caravaggio's younger contemporaries and launched, if it did not start, the painting of the same subject all over the Western world, and particularly in Holland. The over-big head and the dubious expression of the scoundrel may have encouraged the gigantism and bestiality which characterize no little of Italian Seicento painting.

Before we leave the early and earliest phases of Caravaggio's career, we must look at a picture till lately in the Barberini Palace of Rome, but now in the Rohoncz Collection at Lugano (Plate 18).

It represents a young woman kneeling as she leans against a huge, broken wheel. Her eyes are wide open but do not seem to look at anything in particular. Lightly clad above the waist and voluminously draped below, wheel apart, she and her draperies produce a pyramidal effect. The fingers of her right hand touch the blade, while her left rests on, but does not grip, the pommel of a sword. She kneels on a cushion across which lies the martyr's palm. No indication of space.

But for the wheel and the sword and the palm, there is nothing here to suggest a virgin martyr. The good-looking young woman named Catherine perhaps looks as if posing for her portrait, and one is tempted to ask whether that really was not the purpose of the canvas. If we take the bust alone, we are reminded of Giorgionesque heads, and of Palma in particular ; but without the radiance of early Cinquecento. The pose is dramatic enough to suggest a story. She looks anxious.

The figure on the right in both the Fogg
Museum and the Sciarra gambling scenes looks
like a naturalistic study from the model for a
young man getting ready to bestir himself. He
occurs in one of the compositions decorating the
Chapel of S. Luigi dei Francesi in Rome
(Plate 19) ; which was by Caravaggio's contemporaries, and now again, esteemed as his
highest achievement.

The scene, highly dramatic, takes place in
what looks like a gaunt room in a narrow
Venetian alley, lit up not so much by the faint
glimmer reflected from the house opposite and
drifting through a window as by a glare flashed
from the right on the wall and on all the faces.
I remain perplexed as to the source of this light.
Almost it would seem as if it came from above.
Be that as it may, the five individuals of various
ages sitting round a table act as if electrified by
the entry of Christ to call Matthew ; or was it
the sudden dazzle as from a bull's-eye ? And
the wonder seems to have affected their legs as
well as their faces, for these sprawl in unseemly
fashion. Another matter that troubles me is the
length of the pointing arm and the question to
whom it belongs. The charming boy (Plate 20)
is a more attractive version of the one in the

" Soldier and Gypsy " (Plate 14). When Zuccaro, the prince of the then surviving academicians and the most authoritative, was taken to see this canvas, he exclaimed, " Giorgione all over again," so unusual was it in the Italian painting of the time.

Unfortunately no interior by Giorgione has come down to us and we cannot check the statement. This much we can agree to, namely, that if Caravaggio had predecessors in Italy they were Venetians. We find them in the ageing Bellini, as early as the S. Giobbe altarpiece and advanced in the S. Zaccaria one, and more defined in the Carpaccio S. Ursula series, in the canvas representing the reception of the ambassadors or, better still, in the bedchamber (Plates 22, 23).

They do not aim at flooding the entire interior with a blinding flash and at over-obvious contrasts of light and shade, yet they betray a keen interest in the subtle play of chiaroscuro. Only it remains discreet and serves the purpose of the illustrator, the interpreter, and does not, as Caravaggio does in this instance, solicit or even impose admiration of a technical stunt.

As illustration the subject lends itself to familiar treatment. Here it is reduced or, if you

will, transformed into " genre " ; and " genre "
as naked and unashamed as perhaps had never
before appeared in Italy in a sacred subject.
One may go further and say it looks like the
illustration to a detective story. A police magis-
trate makes an apparition at a gambling-den
presided over by a still fine although broken
gentleman (Plate 20).

Opposite in the same chapel is represented the
martyrdom of St. Matthew (Plate 21). I am
at a loss to know where I am, how I got there,
and what I am seeing.

An elderly man lying on the escarped edge of
a pit, presumably in the vaults of a prison, is
seized by a slender nude with a drawn sword.
The startled onlookers scatter, while a winged
child dives down from above with a palm in his
hand.

Much here is conventional. The Giorgionesque group to our left, the academic nudes,
the monumental pre-Piranesi prison, the more
than Correggiesque foreshortening of the angel.
Caravaggio's own is the lighting reflected as from
polished surfaces, but of uncertain substance.
Yet an achievement without rival in the Italy
of that day.

On the altar of the same chapel (Plate 27) we

see the same elderly man, with enfolding and
dangling draperies, stooping over an open codex
with his left knee on a hard stool while turning
to receive the dictation of an angel who hovers
over him with hands emphasizing his words.
This acrobatic performance by a dignified old
man replaced an earlier painting which offended
the taste of the authorities and finally found its
way to the Berlin Museum (Plate 26). The saint
was too plebeian and lacking in decorum, with
one peasant leg swung over the other. I venture
to suspect that what really disturbed them was
the too lightly draped Titianesque angel—more
appropriate to a Venetian idyll—who caressingly
guides the Apostle's hand as he painfully forms
well-shaped Hebrew letters.

These paintings in S. Luigi dei Francesi seem
to have been regarded as his culminating achievement. Admired by younger contemporaries in
the craft as well as by high-placed patrons, they
were greeted with cool reserve in public utterance
by the academicians and probably with no little
private vituperation. Later on, in the second
part of this study, more will be said about the
reaction to Caravaggio's art.

III

We shall now take a look at the other pictures
Caravaggio painted before having to flee from
Rome to knock about as a disenchanted wanderer
till his squalid bitter end as a raging Hercules in
low life.

"The Sacrifice of Isaac" (Plate 29) is now in the
Uffizi, an oblong composition with a Palmesque
landscape and an Abraham who has the same
head as the second St. Matthew (Plate 27), a
head, be it noted, far closer to the types of the
old Bellini and Savoldo than to those of Raphael.
He is as affected about butchering his son as if
he were a Jewish slaughterer ritualistically slay-
ing a sheep. Isaac on the other hand howls with
animal fear. The same kind of incongruity that
we have noted in the case of the vulgar trooper
in the calling of Matthew (Plate 20)—or again
in the too " horned son of toil ", the St. Matthew
now in Berlin, and in the far-fetched action of
the martyrdom of Matthew (Plates 26, 21).

Incongruity, at times malicious incongruity,
henceforth dominated Caravaggio's work in

Rome.   Look for instance at the pair of pictures
in S. Maria del Popolo.

In the one (Plate 30), at first glance, we see
only an old jade and an elderly groom holding
it by the bridle while it kicks up its front leg.   In
the foreground below, we descry, facing away
from us towards the group just mentioned, the
sprawling figure of an officer with arms shot out
in a faint.

We are to interpret this charade as the conversion of Paul.   Nothing more incongruous
than the importance given to horse over rider,
to dumb beast over saint.   Surely more picaresque than holy.   No trace of a miraculous
occurrence of supreme import.[1]

[1] Professor Morassi published in the *Emporium* for March
1947 another version of St. Paul's conversion which he
found in the Balbi Collection at Genoa (Plate 32).   In the
reproduction this work looked to me as if it could be by
Caravaggio.   After inspecting the original I am sure it is
by him ; but it must be of somewhat later date, nearly
contemporary with the Acts of Mercy in the Misericordia
at Naples.

It is romantic and scenic to a degree, and if we were
sure that it was done later might be taken as a palinode to
the callous treatment of the subject in the picture of S.
Maria del Popolo.   And yet, along with the favourite
crossed diagonals of the composition (less obvious than, for
instance, in the " Crucifixion of St. Peter "), there is no
lack of incongruities : the groom who is dealing with the
hysterical horse, instead of being young and alert, is a

Nor is the companion piece (Plate 31) more appropriate to the subject, the lifting of the cross to which Peter is already nailed. But for the noble Titianesque head of the victim, the rest is a study in the raising of a heavy weight without the aid of machinery. Of the chief performers, the one who acts as crane and the other as booster, we see the back of the one and the buttocks of the other. We do not see their faces. No need. They are mere mechanisms.

Hard to conceive a more dehumanized treatment of the subject. No doubt the arrangement of the four figures as crossed diagonals taking up the entire canvas was a happy thought ; but here as in the " Conversion of Paul ", as in most of Caravaggio's other compositions, I find it almost impossible to descry where I am, in what kind of space and with what dimensions.

plumed and majestic patriarch ; the Apostle, whose clothes seem to have been torn to shreds with the violence of his fall, leaving him all but naked, is lying prostrate as he hides his face from the vision which blinded him. One is left uncertain, however, whether this is not merely the automatic reaction against sudden pain. As for the Lord, He is a youngish man of the refined gentlemanly class, that we see in the " Martyrdom of St. Matthew " (Plate 21), in the " Seven Acts of Mercy " (Plate 66) and elsewhere. While with eloquent hands He appeals to Paul, a chubby boy-angel grasps Him around the chest as if to prevent his falling. Bizarre and fascinating !

I have the same complaint to make of the Borghese " Virgin with St. Anne " (Plate 33). A glimmer of light illuminating a background that I could hypnotize myself into imagining was a landscape high above the three figures. The Christ Child is already a boy, a beautiful little male. His mouth is awry with loathing of the serpent—too much as if in bronze—wriggling at His own and His mother's feet. She looks down with anxious interest, but I cannot make out whether she is stooping or getting up from a seat. She is a lady, every inch, but beside her stands her mother, a tall, wizened, hard-featured *ciociara*, a peasant woman of the hill country between Rome and Cassino. Why this contrast, this incongruity ?

The same *ciociara* meets us where she belongs, as the wife of the elderly innkeeper in the Patrizi version, now in the Brera at Milan, of Caravaggio's " Christ at Emmaus " (Plate 34). Again we are left in the dark as to where we are, what space the scene is occupying.

As a composition it is even more lopsided than the last, and the faces almost lime-lit, as are most faces in Caravaggio's mature works. In other respects the subject is handled quietly, soberly, appropriately, with a Christ as little unsatisfactory

as any known to me, and disciples who do not
overdo their amazement. All in all, scarcely
more dramatic than Moretto in the Brescia
Gallery (Plate 35).

The London National Gallery treatment of
the same subject (Plates 36, 38, 39), done perhaps
earlier than the Patrizi picture, would be an
excellent " genre " piece, representing hard-
visaged peasants, humping shoulders, and arms
shot out, who have heard something startling.
The innkeeper might come out of many Spanish
paintings. The still-life on the table has most of
the elements of our artist's earliest works and is
meticulously done. This and much else that is
admirable—but how incongruous with the boy
Christ in their midst ! Why make Him so
young, if not, one is tempted to say, *pour épater
les bourgeois* ! Yet as a painting it is as good as
anything Caravaggio ever did ; nowhere else does
he so closely anticipate Velasquez.

Interesting and amusing to compare this composition with Cézanne's " Card-players " (Plate
37 ; now belonging to Mr. and Mrs. Stephen C.
Clarke of New York) and with the same artist's
still-life with the same geranium pot (Mr. and
Mrs. Samuel A. Levisohn, New York), or with
the still-life piece in the New York Museum of

c.—c

Modern Art, besides many others. How much the Cinquecento artist holds to contour and chiaroscuro and the last great modern to spacing and tactile values ! Note how identical are the compositions. A detailed analysis of what was like and what unlike in these two masterpieces would demand a wide and deep acquaintance with the painters' craft for the three intervening centuries and is quite beyond my competence.

At Messina there is still another and later version of the same theme, but so mauled about that the composition only is discernible (Plate 40). Christ and the two disciples are proved theologians, discussing subtly yet emphatically. It is not likely that the two intruding topers, assuming that they hear and see, could follow the argument. Their unbidden presence is the more incongruous as they overcrowd the composition.

As badly preserved, and likewise in Messina, is the " Incredulity of St. Thomas " (Plate 41), evidently done in the same spirit as the last. Six doctors of theology, intellectually virile, except one who is sniffy with age, discuss Christ's wound as if they were doctors of medicine come together to consult about a clinical case of unusual interest.

Both these canvases are perhaps in what I am tempted to call the posthumous manner of an artist. I mean to say that close followers are apt to carry a creator's style beyond what he himself would have done. He was held back by training under teachers—whether in person or through their works—whose manner he never quite abandoned, as well as by the tact of genius. Followers are given to extracting what is newest in a predecessor and to emphasizing and exaggerating.

How heartless the Messina "Doubting Thomas" compared with the version of the same subject that used to be in the Neues Palais at Potsdam! (Plate 44). The heads, perhaps not quite so intellectual, are solemnly, nobly in earnest, and Thomas with more awe than doubt lets Christ guide his hand to His wound.

As mere composition it is a masterpiece in the Venetian early Cinquecento mode, semicircular, compact yet free, each figure existing as its complete self, while communally concentrated on the same point.

In contrast to this is the "Concert" of the Uffizi (Plate 42),[1] so ruined that it had better

[1] Possibly Caravaggesque rather than by Caravaggio. Momentary opinion would attribute it to Manfredi.

be represented by an old copy there. It is a scattered composition, anticipated by the Bassano rather than the Bellini-Giorgione group painters. It is spread out, " factual " ; nevertheless, a delightfully balanced arrangement with each performer individualized. Note that the gentleman who is taking off his hat as he joins the company is the Matthew of the S. Luigi painting (Plate 19).

As I enjoy frivolous parallels, let me bring to notice a composition of to-day, perhaps its direct descendant, although unaware of its distant ancestor. It is Cadmus's " Greenwich Village Cafeteria " in the New York Museum of Modern Art (Plate 43).

At about the same time Caravaggio must have painted a " Betrayal ", a copy of which Professor Longhi reproduces (*Proporzioni*, I, pl. 16). A Giorgionesque composition that looks as flashy and flimsy as a Pietro della Vecchia.

After writing about the " Virgin with St. Anne ", I could not resist the temptation to talk of the " Christ at Emmaus " where the same old peasant woman appears, and that in turn led me on. Before proceeding to examine Caravaggio's later altarpiece, painted before and after he left Rome, I must turn back and speak

first of the S. Agostino Madonna, then of the
" Entombment " now in the Vatican Gallery,
and finally of his nude or half-nude figures with
the attributes of Eros or David, Narcissus or
Baptist.

The Madonna of S. Agostino, known as the
" Madonna di Loreto " (Plate 47), is the most
graceful and gracious figure of Caravaggio's
that has come down to us. She stands in a
niche, the light streaming in from our left and
lighting her and the Child, and the faces of the
pilgrims kneeling in prayer at her feet. (What a
contrast, so to say, with such a creation of
XIXth-century Catholicism as the Madonna of
Lourdes. *Es lässt tief blicken—cela donne à penser !*)
She stoops towards them, but seems to feel the
burthen of the Holy Child's weight as He
blesses. It is this which I find incongruous and
not, as did contemporaries, the rusticity of the
worshippers and the ugliness of the peasant's feet.
These figures do not shock us, we who know
them in Murillo and got to like them there. In
essentials, however, they are nearer to Velasquez.

Soon after the S. Agostino " Madonna with the
Pilgrims ", the Borghese " Madonna with St.
Anne ", and the Patrizi " Christ at Emmaus ",
Caravaggio may have painted the " Salome with

the Head of the Baptist " (Plate 45), now in the
Escorial, which Professor Longhi brought to
light and exhibited at the Caravaggio show in
Milan. The types of the women are close to
those in the canvases above mentioned, while
the heads of the executioner and of the Baptist
anticipate later works.

The peculiar thing about this picture is the
interpretation. Salome, instead of being a care-
free young girl, proud of the success of her
dancing, looks sad and woebegone and dismally
middle-aged. Even Caravaggio is seldom if
ever again so unexpected, so untraditional, so
incongruous. He anticipates by centuries Jean
Cocteau in his neurasthenic Jocasta or the
founder of the French incongruists, Laforgue, in
his " Moralités Légendaires ".

The Vatican Entombment (Plate 48), which
well into my time was considered, along with
Domenichino's St. Jerome, as one of the greatest
masterpieces of art, is somewhat spoiled for me
by the head of Nicodemus, incongruously huge
and the more distasteful for being conspicuously
in the centre of the scene. Nor to my taste is
the action of the woman with her hands thrown
up in grief, although no doubt she serves to
balance the arm of the Saviour and to give the

arrangement a kind of diagonal twist, held in high esteem by some schools of aesthetic prophets. I keep my admiration for the Magdalen and the beloved disciple, but most of all for the way the dead Christ is being carried. Inspired by Raphael, but realized more convincingly. Where all this is taking place is more than I can guess, nor whence the light. The chiaroscuro playing over John and Magdalen is lyrical.

Rubens copied this Entombment. His picture is now in the Liechtenstein Collection at Vaduz (Plate 49). Let me draw attention to the differences between the two versions.

Note in the first place that Rubens is not copying slavishly and literally but is assimilating and turning a Caravaggio into a Rubens. He omits the woman with her arms thrown up and changes a diagonal to a centralized composition. The Mother is more worldly, and between her and the young man whose right arm holds up the shoulders of the corpse, Rubens, to round off the composition, has slipped in the head of a Titianesque beauty. Note that the females are of a higher social class. Note also that instinctively Rubens realized that he must tell where the action is taking place, and painted a grotto in the background, but he omits the lush plant in the foreground as unlikely to be growing in an utterly sunless pit. One might point out much else that distinguishes a Flemish genius from an almost contemporary Italian. But enough here.

IV

Now for the nudes or half-nudes which Caravaggio painted during these Roman years.

The winged Eros of the Berlin Gallery (Plate 50) snatches his arrows as he rises from his couch and laughs at the thought of all the fun he will have playing with them. The left leg is struggling to get free of the bedclothes, while the right comes down on a floor strewn with odds and ends, pieces of armour, a mouth-organ, a violin, a musical partition, a carpenter's square, a pair of compasses, etc., and above the couch is a crown with rare spikes. Whether these paraphernalia are symbolic or allegorical [1] I know

[1] In the cover now in the National Gallery, Washington, to the Naples Bust of Bernardo de' Rossi painted by

not. What I do know, because I see it clearly before me, is a youthful nude, well-proportioned, firm-fleshed, fine-limbed, in a diagonal pose. He is amused. It will be such a lark to see these silly human bipeds hit by his darts, and going mad with the sweet poison.

The Doria Baptist (Plate 51) is as young and as playful as the Eros. He, too, is diagonally posed as he sprawls at the edge of a sumptuous couch while leaning on his left arm. He looks quizzically at us as he caresses a sheep with his extended right hand. Over him hovers a young eagle. The scene seems placed in the fore-ground of a wilderness. Undoubtedly remini-scent, as indeed is the Eros (although to a less degree), of Michelangelo's youthful nudes in the Sistine Chapel—or perhaps only of those the Carracci were then painting in the Farnese Palace? Artists are more likely to look at what their competitors are doing than at the master-pieces of the past, least of all those of the recent past.

Seen in the most commonplace way, as if by

Lorenzo Lotto in 1505, similar instruments are being played with by a Cupid. It is not probable that Caravaggio was acquainted with this allegorical painting, but the climate (as it were) that produced the one may still have prevailed with the other, nearly a century later.

an artist with no vision, is the Eros of the Pitti Gallery (Plate 52). He is represented as a puffy infant fast asleep in unattractive nakedness. No alleviating surroundings, no cradle, no bed, no room, no landscape. Space is ignored. Only bull's-eye lighting interested the painter. And how incongruous ! This leathery, vulgar brat the Eros, the Cupid, the Amor of myth and rhyme !

Not again as Eros, but as a surly lad sitting diagonally in the fore-edge of a forest, the all-but-nude Baptist of the Spada Palace (Plate 53) looks suspiciously toward our right. His torso and arms are highly lit in contrast with the darkness of the background. The hands are more rigid than elsewhere in Caravaggio's paintings. Curious, by the way, that he either was indifferent or never learned how to paint hands expressively or even accurately.

There exist other treatments of the semi-nude as Baptist. Only one deserves mention here. It is represented by two versions, one at Naples and the superior one, the probable original now in the Museum of Kansas City (Plate 54). Here the Baptist is more grown up, still sits diagonally as in the Spada picture, sits and broods, sits nowhere in particular, his splendidly

beautiful body glimmering out of the blackness.

The contrast between these figures posed as
brooding, gloomy young Baptists or represented
as Bacchus, could tempt one to interpret them as
Pater might have—Pater, the author of " Apollo
in Picardy " and of " Denis de l'Auxerrois ". I
invite the Warburg Institute to apply its methods
to the problem.

It is an easy transition from these moody
young Baptists to the David of the Borghese
(Plate 55). He looks bitterly unhappy as he
brandishes his sword and grasps the head of
Goliath. Youthful but no longer a boy, he
seems sorrowful and hesitating, frightened perhaps by what he has done ; at all events an
uneasy, insecure conqueror. Goliath was supposed to be Caravaggio's portrait of himself—
but of this later. The gleaming body flashes out
of pitch darkness in complete isolation. But
what a head, torso and arm—Lysippian almost !

Here we may mention the " Medusa " of the
Uffizi (Plate 56), a distressing study of a face in
agony. It was admired by the Cavalier Marino,
a friend of Caravaggio's and in their day a
renowned and influential master of versified
conceits.

There is at Vienna (Plate 58) a later " David " done probably, as Professor Longhi believes, in Naples. It is more sculptural than the last, almost Quattrocento in modelling and contours, but not so interesting as interpretation. The Borghese version tempted one to imagine that its painter had vaguely in mind something which centuries later found expression in Hebbel's *Judith*. The picture before us is of a rather stupid hobbledehoy clutching the hair of a decapitated head, scarcely aware of what he has done.

Still another " David " by Caravaggio is known through a contemporary copy now at Madrid (Plate 59). As in the S. Maria del Popolo altarpieces, it ignores the human reaction to what is going on. What we do see are legs almost parallel with the arms glimmering with reflected light, while the profile of the head is hardly legible against the dark background. The youth bends to tie up the hair of Goliath's head. The Philistine's features resemble those in the Borghese picture (Plate 55).

To the same group, despite differences in mood, belongs the " Narcissus " of the Borghese Gallery in Rome (Plate 60). Against blackness the youth is seen resting with hands and knees on the water's edge as he peers into its glassiness. Open-mouthed, he gazes and is spellbound by the reflection. Despite faults of detail (due probably to dirty varnish or repainting), it is a fascinating presentation. Characteristically incongruous is the importance given to the naked knee which all but puts the head in the shade (in literal as well as figurative sense). As a matter of curiosity, let me draw attention to the pattern of the coat on the boy's back. It is identical with the one on the skirt of the Doria " Magdalen " (Plate 13) and must have been on a piece of stuff that remained a studio property for years.

With the pretext of celebrating the martyrdom of Four Saints, Caravaggio painted for S. Andrea da Vinci in Rome an altarpiece with four semi-nudes (Plate 61). It is a study of four male figures seen back to back. When fresh, it may have been beautiful as well as admirable.

With these may be placed the nearly contemporary copy of a Sebastian (Plate 46) that was exhibited in Milan in 1951 (Catal. N/50) as in private hands. The youthful nude looks down amused at his executioner, who binds his calves to a tree-stump. A younger one seems to be fastening the martyr's waist-band behind his back. The incongruity of the Saint's expression is characteristic of Caravaggio.

Among semi-nudes, I would draw attention to the " St. Jerome " of the Borghese Gallery (Plate 62), which may be by Caravaggio. A bald, bearded old man, conning an open book, reaches out absentmindedly toward the inkstand beyond which, on still another open book, lies a skull. A perfect study anatomically, psychologically and as lighting, but as so often with Caravaggio, no space, no atmosphere, no contingence, scarcely more than in the frescoes of the early Christian catacombs.

Another " St. Jerome " from Montserrat in Spain appeared at the Caravaggio exhibition of 1951 (Catal. N/34 ; illustration). It is less dramatic than the last, but finer as a nude.

Finally in this group, and rather early, one may place a painting now in the Wadsworth Atheneum, Hartford, Conn. It represents St. Francis supported by an angel (Plate 63). The figures are lit up against a pitch-black landscape, with glints in the middle distance as of moonlight on water. There is a tenderness in the angel's action and look, worthy of the Byzantine groups portraying the Madonna comforting her Son in a faint—the *anapausis*—a composition which Caravaggio may have seen in Venice. The angel, as a nude, is twin of the Berlin Eros, but probably somewhat earlier. All in all, one of the artist's best achievements, in date as well as in quality belonging to the mood of the Doria " Rest in the Flight ", and like that strongly reminiscent of Tintoretto's idyllic landscapes with figures in the Scuola di San Rocco at Venice.

V

We can now turn to the altarpieces Caravaggio painted just before leaving Rome, then to those in Naples, in Malta, in Siracusa, and finally in Palermo.

The earliest was done for a Roman church. It is the " Death of the Virgin " now in the Louvre (Plate 64). It did not please. The authorities were shocked by the swollen body and the naked feet of the corpse. They were blind to the way the Madonna seems to be asleep with the right arm relaxed in repose, indifferent to the so-dignified, so-earnest, so-pensive company

assembled ; and failed to appreciate the arrangement so architectural and yet so natural.   Deeply
appealing is the young woman in the foreground
broken with grief.

Here again—where does this take place ?
Rafters, a huge curtain, and a diagonal light
which dazzles on bare skulls, on the Virgin's
face, on the mourning female's back and arms.

The types are more Venetian than Roman,
although one head recalls Raphael's St. Paul in
the St. Cecily altarpiece of the Bologna Gallery.

I have less to say in favour of the Vienna
altarpiece known as the " Rosary Madonna "
(Plate 65).   The kneeling figures are admirable,
but a gifted artist like Caravaggio could scarcely
have painted a duller, more academic picture.

It seems that this work was done in Naples,
whence it migrated quickly, perhaps because it
found no friends there.   Caravaggio painted
other pictures for Neapolitan churches, where
they still exist ; but it is difficult to descry them
through the grime which now befouls them.

Even the most visible, the " Seven Acts of
Mercy " (Plate 66), in the church of the Misericordia, is barely legible.   One makes out two
embraced angels swooping down with the
Madonna framed by their wings, the naked back

of a reclining man, a woman with a frightened
look giving suck to a greybeard—the story of a
daughter saving her imprisoned father from
starvation—a surpliced clerk with a burning
torch accompanying a corpse that is being
transported, Giorgionesque figures as in the
" Martyrdom of Matthew at S. Luigi " in Rome
(Plate 21), and a fine portrait head. The angels
surpass Correggio for invention and boldness of
action.

The " Flagellation " at S. Domenico (Plate 67)
now looks like a somewhat dramatized variant of
Sebastiano del Piombo's fresco at S. Pietro in
Montorio in Rome. The bald-headed executioner is of disproportionate length and the other
is deliberately bestial, as occurs too often in
the works of Caravaggio's followers but seldom
in his own. The bending figure is almost a
repetition of the Madrid " David " (Plate 59).
And yet, if we ignore these errors of interpretation
and look at these figures for their tactile values
and movement, no Italian painting of the
Quattrocento surpasses it—not even Antonio
Pollajuolo's various nudes.

During his sojourn at Malta, so brilliantly begun
and so tempestuously ended, Caravaggio painted
a number of pictures, two of which are still there.

C.—D

In S. Giovanni at La Valletta (Cappella
d'Italia) there is a St. Jerome (Plate 68), less
broken with age, far less contrite, more like the
manly figures in the Messina " Incredulity of
Thomas ". He reclines naked to below the waist
and writes in an open book. Beyond it is a skull.
This last and the nude form a pyramid of
reflected light. Coming whence and going
whither ?

It has been observed that the head of this
St. Jerome reminds one of the Olaf de Wigancourt, Grand Master of the Knights of Malta,
whose portrait he painted at the same time
(Plate 76). It is not surprising, for a painter
cannot get rid quickly of the visual image that
has been preoccupying him. If the portrait was
painted first, something of it would reappear in
the next picture. There remains a possibility
that a certain likeness was actually intended.

The " Beheading of the Baptist " (Plate 69)
is almost as austere a composition as Andrea del
Sarto's fresco of the same subject at the Scalzi in
Florence. In a prison yard, in front of a deep
arch, a pyramidal group of five figures. The
executioner bends over the decapitated Baptist
to pick up his head. Opposite, Herodias bends
to receive it, while between them an old woman

grasps her own head in her hands with horror, and an officer points to the basin. This officer reminds me of one in Lotto's " Martyrdom of St. Stephen " in the Bergamo Gallery, that master's most Giorgionesque composition. Herodias bends like the Prado David (Plate 59). Finally let me add that excepting the " Calling of Matthew " (Plate 19) this is the only Caravaggio known to me that tells me where I am.

As homicide drove Caravaggio from Rome, arrogant brawling drove him from Malta, and he took refuge in Sicily, first in Siracusa. There for S. Lucia alla Marina (Plate 70) he painted the burial of the saint to whom that church was dedicated. Under a bare wall pierced by an arch, towering high over the figures, the youthful corpse lies stretched out with the head thrown back. There are mourners with impressively convincing attitudes and gestures. There is a bishop blessing. Far more prominent than the rest are three figures on the fore-edge, more than twice the size of the others : one brutally digging, one in armour, and a third bending over with a grand display of buttocks. Almost cynical in its incongruity is the reduction of the mourners to background figures and the gross importance given to the material fact. There was a beginning of this in Tintoretto, the merest beginning, and (by the way) the bending giant reminds me of one in Pordenone's fresco of the Magi at Treviso.

At Messina, Caravaggio painted a number of pictures. Two certainly his remain in the museum of that town : a " Raising of Lazarus " and an "Adoration of the Shepherds ".

Lazarus (Plate 71), still a rigid and—be it noted—naked corpse, has been dragged out of a grave, a grave under the pavement ; he is addressed with a gesture of command by the Saviour, while the spectators gape and an old woman kisses him and a young one looks on feelingly. The figures are known to us from previous works of the master, including the Saviour, who repeats the not-too-impressive gesture He has in the " Calling of Matthew " (Plate 20). The light falls on the nude and his attendant, and comes from the left into a space that seems to be bounded by high verticals. The grouping to both sides of the four central figures is as remarkable as are the diagonals and parallels.

A rare treatment is the complete nakedness of Lazarus, who elsewhere appears swaddled in grave-clothes. Another singularity is that instead of being revived while standing inside an upright sepulchre out-of-doors, Lazarus has been pulled up from a grave under a pavement—for burial under the floor of churches was the usage in Italy till some few generations ago. For this I recall but one precedent. It was in a fresco by Pordenone at Collalto destroyed during the first world war (Plate 72).

The other altarpiece is a Nativity (Plate 73) originally perhaps a noble work, not unworthy to stand by Sebastiano del Piombo's sublime "Pietà" at Viterbo, which indeed may have inspired it. Under the flat thatch of a shed, the Virgin coiffed like a peasant woman reclines on her right elbow while the Holy Child clingingly kisses her. Two elderly and two younger men, all stately, approach and gaze with reverent wonder. The light from the front is reflected from all the figures, leaving the surroundings dim. Ass and ox barely discernible in middle distance. Pose and action of the Madonna may be reminiscent of Byzantine compositions. It is a work without blemish, without a touch of incongruity. But iconographically it is singular. The two elders have the grave intellectual aspect of distinguished theologians. Only the half-nude younger man could be taken for a shepherd.

Yet they are unlikely to have been meant for kings.

Finally, there is a " Nativity " in the Oratory of S. Lorenzo at Palermo (Plate 74). In a dark shed crouches the Madonna over the Child who lies on the floor facing her. (He recalls the " Eros " of the Pitti Gallery (Plate 52).) Joseph turns around to draw a shepherd's attention to the Infant. Next to the rustic stands a Capuchin friar with clasped hands. On the other side of the Virgin a young deacon stoops to gaze. These two are meant for Francis and Lawrence. Above them an angel swoops down, pointing upward and flaunting a ribbon with the inscription " Gloria in Excelsis Deo ".

These figures flash out of the gloom as does the spot-lighted angel, the Virgin, and the legs and thighs only of Joseph. These by the way are too firm and fleshy, while shoulders and head are too alert for his putative age. A relatively young Joseph—what an incongruity ! Yet a wonderful work. Pity it was his last !

VI

A word about Caravaggio's portraits. Early
writers mention a number, but portraiture could
scarcely have attracted him. It gave few oppor-
tunities for displays of chiaroscuro and delight in
incongruity. People, in those primitive days of
art-ignorance, wanted above all a likeness that
satisfied their friends, and not to be regarded as
subjects for laboratory-treatment in the fields of
pictorial technique and exotic pattern. The
few portraits that have come down to us look
as if their painter was bored to produce mere
resemblance, and revenged himself by making
them prosaic and dull. Only when he could
treat them as heads peeping out in altarpieces,
as in the Rosary one at Vienna, are they more
spirited.

A great artist, and Caravaggio surely was one,
could scarcely be less interesting than in his
" Cardinal Maffei ", his " Pope Paul V " or even
his Berlin " Young Woman " (Plate 75). They
are as commonplace as the less-inspired effigies
of the so-talented but so-provincial G. B. Moroni

of Bergamo, and no better than Scipione Pulzone's
" Young Woman with a Book in her Hand "
(formerly Barberini Collection), or less prosaic
than the same artist's " Family Group " in the
Colonna Gallery.

The one exception is the " Portrait of Olaf de
Wigancourt ", Grand Master of the Knights of
Malta (Plate 76). He stands full length in complete armour, looking to our right, the com-
mander's baton held with both hands. His
helmet is carried by a page. Attitude and
expression of kindly manliness on the part of the
master, and of innocence on the part of the page.
All in all, the presentation not only of distinguished but of finely humanized individuals.
Yet, although the concept and pose and placing
are so much after the pattern invented by
Titian, this painting, an undoubted masterpiece, yet lacks a something, a beam of
glamour that radiates from the great Venetian's
portraits.

I said just now that his best portraits peep out
of his altarpieces. There is one in Messina in
such bad state that we hesitate to give it an
attribution. Yet it may have been by Caravaggio (Plate 77). It represents Pilate showing
Christ to the Jews. I shall not attempt to

discuss the attribution or to appreciate it as the masterpiece that originally it may have been. It suffices to point to Pilate as an obvious likeness and perhaps more than any other of his paintings worthy of a great portraitist. It would have suited Caravaggio's humour to find somebody to sit for that character.

We now have examined as many of Caravaggio's paintings as seems worth while.[1] If one or more are omitted that should be accepted, or included that ultimately will not remain in the canon of his works, it will make no appreciable difference to our idea either of his artistic personality or his career as a painter, as an innovator,

[1] Professor Longhi in *Proporzioni*, I, pl. 24, has discovered in Marseilles the picture of a woman reclining with hands folded under her bosom and mouth fallen open. She reminds one of the Lazarus in the Messina picture, and Professor Longhi rightly regards it as a copy after a lost original by Caravaggio and as a Magdalen. If so, it is another instance of the painter's preference for the incongruous. Arthur von Schneider in *Caravaggio und die Niederländer*, p. 134, fig. 37, ascribes this Magdalen to Finsonius and says it is dated 1613.

Another version, in the D. Santiago Alorda Collection at Barcelona, is inscribed as follows : " *Imitando Michaelem | Angelum Carrava . . . | Mediolan | Wibrandus de Geest | Friesius | A⁰ 1620* " (Mostra del Caravaggio, Sansoni, Firenze, 1951, No. 99).

as a troubler of stagnant waters in his own time and as a subject for study in ours.

We shall now proceed to say something about all these matters. But first a word about Caravaggio's drawings and the colour of his paintings as they now appear.

It is perhaps not without significance that not a single drawing is known that can safely be attributed to Caravaggio. Zahn reproduces two sketches, one in black chalk and the other with black chalk and indian ink, that could have been dashed off by almost any follower of Michelangelo Buonarroti, emancipated from manual as well as mental inhibitions.

In the Thomas Lloyd Collection at Lockinge House, Wantage, Berks, there is, or was, a small leaflet with a sketch in indian ink (Plate 78) that corresponds in design with the Sciarra card-sharpers (Plate 17). As draughtsmanship it is feeble, timid even, and probably done by a copyist. If by Caravaggio himself, it would lead us to conclude that he drew much better with his brush than with his pen, and that, like the majority of Venetians who influenced him, he was a born painter rather than draughtsman.

As to the colour of his still-extant works—with the exception of the Louvre " Soldier and

Gypsy " (Plate 14) and the Doria " Rest in the Flight " (Plate 11)—it has not only darkened and lost all lustre, but become confused and dull. I confess that, time and again, I get more out of good photographs of these works than from the originals.

PART II

Having looked at each of Caravaggio's more important works with what light assiduous study of Italian art has provided, I shall now attempt to draw conclusions about his formation, character and quality as craftsman and creator, and proceed to discuss the effects he had on contemporaries as well as on immediate successors. I shall follow with a bit of controversy over the way he has been and is being written about nowadays by German-minded authors, and end by a protest against ignoring aesthetic values in favour of general history and its interests, and worse still of mere antiquarian research, when treating of works of art.

I

Out of habit (bad habit, I grant) I begin with
an inquiry into Caravaggio's origins.

Born and presumably brought up in Caravaggio, his nearest market-towns and shopping-
centres were Bergamo and Cremona. He seems
to have frequented little the first of these, for the
only sign of possible acquaintance with any of
its paintings is, as we have seen, in the Malta
" Beheading of the Baptist " (Plate 69), where
the figure of the commanding officer parallels one
in a " Stoning of Stephen " by Lotto.[1] Both,
however, may have taken him independently
from some work of Giorgione now lost. On the

[1] It may be argued that Caravaggio's naturalistic treatment of feet may have been suggested by Lotto's St.
Joseph in the San Bernardino altarpiece at Bergamo ;
conventional compared with Giovanni Bellini's in his early
" Transfiguration " now in the Museo Civico of Venice.
(Curious, by the way, how archaic artists—and the young
Bellini was nothing if not archaic—took to a naturalistic
treatment of feet. Was it perhaps so much easier to draw
their shapes and bones ?) Possibly Caravaggio's swooping
angels in his Naples " Seven Acts of Mercy " may also be
vaguely and remotely reminiscent of Lotto's S. Bartolommeo
altarpiece.

other hand, Pordenone's frescoes in the cathedral and Giulio Campi's altarpieces in the churches of Cremona seem to have left their impression on him. And he could have known and probably did know Pordenone's frescoes at Piacenza and Corte Maggiore, as well. He may have seen and learned something from Calisto's rather naturalistic paintings in the Incoronata at Lodi. As a matter of fact, wherever in the neighbourhood he looked at paintings, they were apt to be Venetian. His own, executed in Rome soon after his twentieth year, seem to show signs of acquaintance with Venetic masters like Savoldo and Romanino at Brescia, Mantegna at Vicenza, and above all with the great Venetians themselves, the old Bellini, Carpaccio probably, Giorgione and Titian of course, Palma and, above all, Tintoretto. The romantic costumes, the type of virile and thoughtful elderly men, even his chiaroscuro, may be traced back to Venetian sources. He may have seen the Bassano as well, for with them he has many affinities, not only in lighting but in a taste for a bourgeois workaday treatment of sacred subjects.

On his way to Rome he may have stayed in Bologna, and seen Niccolò dell' Abate's charming frescoes in the palace that now serves as Univer-

sity. In and near Rome, not even Michelangelo,
let alone Raphael, seems to have affected him as
much as Sebastiano del Piombo with the Viterbo
" Pietà " and the S. Pietro in Montorio " Flagellation ". In works like the Potsdam " Incredulity of Thomas " (Plate 44), he is so much
a Venetian of the early XVIth century that one
is reminded of the most baffling of problems in
attribution : the Pitti " Three Ages ", which
traditionally went under the name of Lorenzo
Lotto. Indeed, it will not be surprising if one
fine day an attempt is made to assign this
fascinating masterpiece to Caravaggio.

It goes without saying that Caravaggio may
have been unaware of these debts to Venice,
debts which we trace in Linnaean fashion as if
we were studying the relation of plant to plant.
We can assert, with perhaps more conviction,
that[he deliberately turned his back on what he
saw was being painted in Rome. He struck out
for himself, partly because he could not help it,
because it suited his gifts and his formation,
because it was his way, in short ; but also perhaps to display his indifference to what was being
done in Rome. Possibly he enjoyed being
different, being original, and disposed to *épater
les bourgeois*. It might be inferred that it amused

C.—E

him to make people's flesh creep and to get
himself talked about. If so, he was among the
first to indulge what since, among English-speak-
ing people particularly, has been admired,
entertained and petted under the rubric of
" artistic temperament ".

In what as artistic personality was he different
from others who were painting in Rome during
his sojourn there ?

In the first place he ignored the vocabulary and
the phrasing, I mean the types and attitudes
based chiefly on Raphael, that then were current.
Employing Venetic and Venetian figures in
Rome was by itself an innovation, an otherness.
Then, as we have seen again and again, he
enjoyed introducing incongruities, as an offset
perhaps to the *style noble*, to the graceful, to the
pretty, the sentimental, the sugary, that were in
vogue at the time. He liked to insert an ultra-
naturalistic type of low life, a jerky, hunching
tough (for instance) into the midst of other
figures so tactfully and subtly stylized as to look
aristocratic, with carriage and gesture formal and
never casual, that we see in his " Calling of
Matthew " (Plate 20). This led him to launch,
if not to invent, the picaresque motifs that we
find in his card-parties, dominated by a sharper

(Plates 16, 17), his jail-birds behind prison bars in the " Beheading of the Baptist " (Plate 69), even his " Magdalen " (Plate 13).

Except for the " Calling of Matthew " (Plate 20), which even to-day, and in its present state, reminds me of Rembrandt's treatment of light and shade in compositions like the " Night Watch ", Caravaggio's chiaroscuro no longer impresses us. It is too obviously inspired by technical interest and ends by producing melodramatic effects as of sudden illumination by a bull's-eye lantern or a flashlight. Those who enjoy these aspects of painting can find more complete satisfaction in works of the mid-XVth century, like King Réné's *Livre du Cueur d'Amour espris* (now in Vienna), or of the late Bassano (for instance, a " Mocking of Christ " now in Melbourne (Plate 79)), and better still in the recently rediscovered and momentarily so-admired Georges de La Tour.

Velasquez, Vermeer van Delft, and Rembrandt have learnt from him, but shunned his exaggerations, the excesses of the innovator. Velasquez in " Las Meniñas " and " Las Hilandaras ", Rembrandt in scores of masterpieces, Vermeer in his Czernin " Studio " as in most of his canvases, use the effects Caravaggio seems to

have had in mind with a discretion, an avoidance
of technical stunts, a subordination to composition and all its requirements, that Caravaggio
never approached, never even seems to have
envisaged. He flashes a wedge of light into an
indeterminate surface, perhaps a wall, perhaps a
ceiling, but he seldom tells us where we are,
where the scene is being enacted, in what kind of
space, of what dimensions. Although his " Rest
in the Flight " and his " Sacrifice of Isaac "
(Plates 11, 29) betray a fine feeling for landscape, he shuns it, and with the rarest exceptions
prefers indoors to out-of-doors. When out-of-
doors, he avoids depth, either by confining the
scene to a foreground, or by painting it almost
invisibly dark.

Caravaggio makes room for each figure indi-
vidually and in relation to the other figures, but
to space as space he is more than indifferent,
positively averse, one is tempted to think. If
not hostile, then as unaware of it almost as a
Greek vase-painter during the adolescence, or as
a catacomb-dauber during the decrepitude of
Antique art. As unawareness in his day was
improbable, it would seem as if he ignored space
intentionally.

In the present condition of most of his works,

it is difficult to speak of Caravaggio as a colourist.
He shows no little aptitude for colour, as we have
seen in the Doria "Flight" (Plate 11), in the
Louvre "Soldier and Gypsy" (Plate 14), here
and there in the St. Matthew series at S. Luigi
dei Francesi (Plates 19-21, 27). Certain heads
in the martyrdom of the saint may have been
(when less darkened than now) as subtly
coloured within the play of light and shade as
if by Giorgione himself. He tended, however,
particularly during his Roman years, to sacrifice
this, and spiritual significance also, to an exorbi-
tant interest in realizing the single human
shapes, not as the Quattrocentists had done,
principally with outline and contour, but with
the shadows, with stunts of chiaroscuro. He
wanted the figures to be as crystalline as in
Mantegna, yet to emerge startling from a depth
of murky circumfusion, instead of the clear
ground that we see them against in XVth-
century paintings down to the Sistine Ceiling
of Michelangelo—the Michelangelo whom he
parallels in an exclusive preference for the
figure, to landscape and to other surroundings.
Perhaps it is because of this procedure that at
times his nudes, with the light reflected from their
bodies, look as if seen not directly but as in a

mirror, without the warmth of actuality. The light, glancing away from what it illuminates, draws the painter's effort and spectator's attention away from what in art makes for reality, the sense of the bone and muscle and sinew, of grasp and grip of hand, and tread of foot.

Something of all this may account for his failing to persuade, to convince, to impress, as Vermeer and Velasquez and Rembrandt do ; not to speak of the great Venetians to whose shapes he was always turning back. He seemed unaware that with his technique it was an impossible aim ; and the same prepossession with chiaroscuro dimmed the manifestation of his mastery of the nude. But few, if any, Italian painters after Michelangelo surpassed him.

Now for a few words about Caravaggio as an illustrator, that is to say, as a visual interpreter of the themes he was treating.

We have seen, while examining each of his paintings, that he could be a lover of still-life, of things in themselves, for their own qualities and virtues, no matter how familiar and how humble : a wickerwork basket, flowers, leafage, or musical instruments of every kind ; books open or closed. He lost no occasion to introduce them into a composition as the garland of his " Bacchus ", the musical instruments, the carpenter's tools in his " Eros Triumphant ", the bread-basket in both the Patrizi and the National Gallery versions of " Christ at Emmaus " (Plates 5, 50, 34, 36).

Genre painting treats human beings in their workaday situations and activities, as so much still-life, and in the past, the master of the one was also the master of the other, as was supremely the case with Vermeer and Chardin. So when as a recent arrival in Rome, Caravaggio was painting the fruit and flower pieces now in the Ambrosiana and in the Kress Collection (Plates 1, 2), he was busy with genre studies like the " Boy bitten by a Lizard " (Plate 8), the " Fruit-seller " (Plate 4), the " Youth peeling a Pear " (Longhi, *Proporzioni*, I, Plates 8, 9), all of which, even the last-named (of which copies only exist), are as admirable in action as in expression.

Little more than genre is the Hermitage " Lute Player " (Plate 10), so absorbed, so contented, listening and enjoying. From this figure the others like the " Bacchus " and the " Eros Triumphant " are but a step. The step, however,

is important. It is from a representation of
limited, workaday life (no matter how discreetly,
how daintily, how charmingly executed) to one
which as illustration goes beyond—beyond into
the realms of spiritual significance. The allur-
ingly uncanny Bacchus, the winged Eros laughing
for joy like a happy child as he unwinds himself
from bedclothes and starts the day with a sheaf
of arrows in his hand, not only delight us in and
for themselves, but waft us away into worlds of
wonder, of reflection and doubt (Plates 5, 50).
So do the various Baptists he and his closest
followers painted, the Dionysiac one of the Doria
Gallery, and the moody, sulky one of Palazzo
Spada. So in a sense the Borghese " David "
takes one a distance away from the self-contained
object visible before us (Plates 51, 53, 54, 55).

The " David " has led us up to the religious
subjects treated by Caravaggio. We have already
discussed at length and referred again and
again to the paintings at S. Luigi dei Francesi
(Plates 19–21, 27). I cannot say much in their
favour as suitable representations of the events
treated. We criticized the " Calling of Matthew " (Plate 20), his masterpiece and most
admired innovation, for sacrificing too much to
technical problems, for making it too much of

a cabaret-scene and for inserting one figure too naturalistically common, vulgar even, for a decently frequented public-house. In the " Matthew Writing " (Plate 27), we noted the incongruity of the stately elder with one knee on a wooden stool as if he had jumped out of bed to dash off a happy thought or phrase before it escaped him. Incongruous, surely, yet worse was to come. At S. Maria del Popolo, the " Conversion of Paul " (Plate 30) becomes the picture of a horse quietening down after a fright, while the " Crucifixion of Peter " (Plate 31) is degraded to a study of buttocks in a composition of crossed diagonals. Buttocks again in his " Burial of St. Lucy " (Plate 70) and yet again in the " Madonna of Loreto " (Plate 47). Indeed, he seems to have anticipated the sculptors of our day for whom buttocks rather than faces are the most interesting part of the human body. Our artists may find an excuse in the fact that the part of our anatomy that is spiritually the least important is plastically the easiest to render, the most likely to suggest or even to communicate tactile values. (How seldom they succeed !) This could scarcely have been Caravaggio's intention. One must conclude that he enjoyed incongruity and deliberately played for it in his compositions. We find it again in its cruder aspects in the " Raising of Lazarus " (Plate 71), where the corpse sways between falling and standing, and in the Marseilles copy of a serving-wench as a Magdalen. No less incongruous, if not so vulgar, is the London National Gallery version of the " Christ at Emmaus " (Plate 36), where the Saviour, against all tradition and precedents, becomes a boy-preacher, startling yokels out of their wits. In the " Burial of St. Lucy " (Plate 70) you would think the grave-diggers were the real subject of the altarpiece. The funeral is shunted into the middle distance. In the Madrid " David " (Plate 59) attention is absorbed by the legs and arms in parallel arrangement, while the head in deep shadow is scarcely discernible.

It would be easy to discover other incongruities in Caravaggio's paintings. Enough have been cited to make it more than probable that he deliberately introduced incongruous elements into sacred and exalted subject. He was tired of the *style noble*, of grandiosity, of trying to pull oneself up by one's boot-straps, and revolted. In a great artist like Cervantes this feeling led to sublimely luminous and even nostalgic reaction ; in a smaller one, to jeering at one's former gods and sneering at the forms wherewith they were worshipped.

And what shall we say of compositions like his " Acts of Mercy " (Plate 66), where we see the feet only of a corpse taken to burial, a frantic young woman giving her breast to an old man, Giorgionesque figures unintelligibly active, and a man, presumably a doctor, holding up to the light the contents of a glass? All this crowded into a murky interior. Original enough surely, incongruous, almost grotesque ; yet somehow fascinating.

It is a pity that this artistic personality was cut off in its prime. Caravaggio's last paintings are freest from blemishes. While still in Rome, he painted the " Death of the Virgin " (Plate 64), a work in which I find little to criticize. On the contrary, it is one of the best representations of the subject that mature European art has produced, and is admirable not only for the stately solemnity of the figures but for the arrangement as well. The Malta " Beheading of the Baptist " (Plate 69) is a rendering of the severest classical order, reminding us of Andrea del Sarto's most Michelangelesque works, his monochrome frescoes in the Scalzi at Florence. The " Nativity " (Plate 73) leaves one perplexed to

know whether the worshippers are shepherds of
the neighbourhood or kings from the ancient
East. Their dress would make you take them
for the one and their looks for the other. The
lighting, the types and arrangement lead one to
fancy that Sebastiano del Piombo would have
treated this subject as romantically, had he
painted it with the feeling of his Viterbo " Pietà ".

In every successful effort to say things—in no
matter what realm of art, whether verbal, visual
or musical—there are two elements. There is
the idea, the vision, the humming, and there is
the technique of shaping and forming it so that
it becomes sufficiently crystallized to present it to
others.

So in every work of art and in the number of
them that constitutes an aitistic personality, one
may ask how much is new as concept, and how
much is merely a new way, a new technique, a
new palette, a new vocabulary and phrasing, a
new sonority in expressing what has already been
told before, and before, and before.

A new notation is not a new vision. A fresh
way of presenting the commonplace, the workaday, may amuse the public, stimulate young

practitioners and excite the enthusiasm of the
oracular writers on art.   Yet, unless the approach
is new and the realization adequate, no otherness
of technique, of vocabulary, of calligraphy, of
palette, of sonority, will save the product from
being merely of the day for which it was produced, and little more than current journalism.
Later on it may still be referred to in footnotes,
or rouse the condescending benevolence of
curiosity-hunters, but scarcely survive as art, as
a possession for all time.

Refraining from the pleasure it would be to
develop this matter at adequate length—matter
for a big book !—and avoiding the sore temptation of applying the two last paragraphs to the
visual, verbal and musical arts of the last thirty
years, let us see how it affects our valuation of
Caravaggio.

I doubt whether it can be said that he brought
a new visual world into being, as Giotto and
Botticelli, Leonardo and Michelangelo, Mantegna
and the Bellini, Giorgione and his prolongation
Titian, Perugino and Raphael, Correggio and
Parmigianino and Andrea del Sarto and even
Pontormo, even Bronzino had done before him,
not to speak of Paolo Veronese and Tintoretto.
Nor of later and latest like Rubens or Velasquez

or Poussin or Watteau or Tiepolo or David or Ingres or Manet or Degas or Toulouse-Lautrec or Cézanne. If at the sword's point I had to find a recent parallel to Caravaggio, it would be no other than Courbet. Neither could reject the comparison.

His chiaroscuro apart, his figures and faces and heads go back to Bellini and Giorgione and Tintoretto. His nudes seem to have the proportions of Giorgione's Judith (Hermitage) and the frescoes that used to be on the Fondaco dei Tedeschi. In every way Caravaggio makes on one like myself the impression of an early Cinquecento Venetian out of his time, out of his place and—out of his technique.

II

Questions of attribution apart, I have done my best to discover what as artist Caravaggio can still mean to one to-day, how he can still delight, stimulate, life-enhance us. Now that our mind is made up, it will be interesting to

inquire first what his exact contemporaries and
their successors made of him and then, and later
on, what a certain kind of art criticism of our
own day makes of him.

The first full story of Caravaggio's life and the
first criticism of his art was published some sixty
years after his death. It was written by Bellori,
the Vasari of XVIIth-century Italy (Rome,
1672), and seems based on reliable tradition. I
paraphrase the passage (p. 204) that tells most
to our purpose :

" Caravaggio became better known every day
through the new colour-scheme which he was
employing. Not as hitherto soft, and obtained
with few tints, but all based on bold dark strokes
and using black a great deal for giving relief to
his figures. He became so enamoured of his
technique, that he never placed a figure out of
doors in the sun, but put it in a tight-shut room
with the light streaming down from above,
plumb on the prominent parts of an object,
leaving the rest in the shade, so as to give overpowering force to his chiaroscuro. The painters
who then were working in Rome, the young ones
particularly, were taken by this novelty, gathered
around him, and sang his praises as the one and
only imitator of nature. Admiring his works as

if miraculous, they vied with one another as to who should follow him closest in denuding the model (*spogliando il modello*) and in the use of flashing lights. Concerning themselves no longer about learning and instruction, each and all found teachers in the streets and market-places, examples in what they could see there with their own eyes and copy straight from nature. This facilitation attracted the young, but old painters, accustomed to academic methods, were alarmed by this new passion for nature, and never stopped raging against Caravaggio and his procedure. They declared everywhere that he did not know how to come out of cellars, that he was poor in invention, inelegant in drawing and that, without understanding his craft, he painted the figures with one light and on one plane without transitions (*senz' arte coloriva tutte le sue figure ad un lume e sopra un piano senza digradarle*)."

A few pages later the same writer goes on to say : " Undoubtedly Caravaggio came at a time when painting needed him. Nature was disregarded ; figures were done by rote and tradition (*di pratica e di maniera*), more pleasing to a taste for prettiness than to a sense of fact. Brushing aside daintiness and silliness of colour, he reinvigorated the tints, he gave them back

lifeblood and freshness, and admonished painters
to return to the imitation of nature. . . . He
professed such fidelity to the model, that he never
made a stroke with his brush which was not
nature's. He disdained doctrine and insisted
that the greatest art was to owe nothing to
art. . . . Nobody else's painting interested him.
He was the only faithful imitator of nature.
Yet much was wanting in him. He lacked invention, he had no elegance, draughtsmanship,
no learning ; and without the model before his
eyes he was lost. All the same, many fell in love
with his procedure and embraced it eagerly ;
for without study and preparation it allowed
them to copy things as they were in nature,
ordinary and without beauty. Caravaggio
dethroned art and authorized everybody to do
as he pleased. There followed a contempt for
things in themselves beautiful, a total disregard
of the Antique and of Raphael. For the con-
venience of the models and in order to do a head
naturalistically, painters abandoned historical
subjects, the crown of their art, and took to half-
lengths, previously seldom in fashion. This was
followed by the reproduction of rubbishy things
and of deformities, which they paint with
anxious care. Thus if they have to do a piece

C.—F

of armour, they choose the rustiest, if a vase, one
chipped and without a rim. Their clothes are
not drapery but stockings, breeches, bonnets.
In copying figures they devote minute attention
to the wrinkles of the face, the blemishes in the
skin, to knotty fingers and to members deformed
by disease."

Thus wrote a scion of the academic tradition,
who tried to deal fairly with Caravaggio the
painter ; and, I venture to say, with a considerable measure of success. Later on we shall see
what he had to say about him as a human being.

To-day, Caravaggio's fidelity to the model, his
never making a stroke with his brush that was
not nature's, and that " without the model
before him he was lost ", is less manifest than it
was to Bellori and contemporaries. Except for
his chiaroscuro, to which we have referred again
and again, I have discovered naturalistic subjec-
tion to the model only in hunching young toughs
like the one in the " Calling of Matthew "
(Plate 20). Elsewhere I find it seldom and in his
later works, from the " Death of the Virgin "
(Plate 64) to the Palermo altarpiece (Plate 74),
it would be difficult to descry closer attention to
the model than in the " Mannerists " of his day.

How can one execute altarpieces and other

figure compositions from the model with every brush-stroke corresponding exactly to what was there ?   The artist must harness his imagination, and that uses not the model but memory and training, no matter how acquired, whether in schools or self-taught, and of course his experiences and practice as a craftsman, and inevitably his unconscious habits of visualizing.   Only the ungifted but vainly aspiring painter wants the model constantly before him.   He seldom becomes aware that he is looking at it not with his own eyes but with the eyes of his masters.

Furthermore, in the case of Caravaggio, his later paintings—surely among his best—were done in conditions in which he scarcely could have had models, or even assistants.   Driven by the furies, and the fear of the enemies he made of friends, he shows what the spontaneous artist could do when working at top speed.   In these late altarpieces he is in types and composition no less traditional than " mannerists " like the Muzianos or the Zuccaris.   The gravity and the majesty of these works is scarcely more affected by his tricks of chiaroscuro and his sly incongruities, than a High Mass by the babble of a petulant child.

As youth is always taken by innovations, it did not fail to be captivated by Caravaggio.   Are we

not alive to witness the like nowadays, those of
us who see with the eyes and with the ears, as
men of letters particularly are apt to do ?
Caravaggio found an admirer, defender and
propagandist in the person of the most worshipped
versifier of his day ; worshipped not only in
Italy, but in France as well : the famous Cavalier
Marino, known even in what then was barbarous
England, but already producing poetry that not
language only would have prevented his under-
standing.   Marino introduced him to prelates, to
great gentlemen, to cardinals, to the Pope himself, all of whom patronized and employed him.
When more reluctant ecclesiastics hesitated to
accept work Caravaggio did for them, there was
a nobleman or prince ready to take it off
their hands, as was the case with the first version
of the St. Matthew (Plate 26) purchased by
Giustiniani, and the " Death of the Virgin "
(Plate 64) bought on Rubens' recommendation
by the Duke of Mantua.   (This last picture, by
the way, unwelcome to those who had ordered it,
could not leave Rome without being shown to
crowds who came to admire it.   Afterwards it
passed with most of the Mantua pictures to King
Charles I of England.)

We can understand that the emancipation

from the academy, from the *style noble* and the almost dandified prettiness of the painters who enjoyed honour and emoluments when Caravaggio came to Rome, should have delighted *les jeunes* ; and further still freed them from the pitiless labour of learning to draw (unless, like Raphael or Ingres or Picasso, they were born draughtsmen) and replaced it with the expeditious procedure of sensational chiaroscuro. All that we readily understand. Not so easily that the leaders of high society should take him up as they did. Perhaps they too were bored not only with the style then current, but with the subject-matter, and were delighted to change over to scenes of genre, of low-life, of subjects that bordered on the grotesque and even the vulgar, as Spanish grandees were already enjoying picaresque stories, and presently were to enjoy paintings that paralleled them.

Perhaps still another element counted with the upper classes : Caravaggio's mischievous delight in incongruity. Many instances of it were pointed out while we were examining his paintings one by one. They amused and delighted, as T. S. Eliot, James Joyce and Gertrude Stein have amused and delighted in our day. The first founded his terraqueous popularity

on the incongruities of his early verses with
their adolescent sneers and jeers at life and art
and the maliciously ludicrous transpositions of
tags from the poets whom generous youth was
supposed to love. Joyce kept re-writing his
Portrait of the Artist as a Young Man in language
more and more and ever more at the mercy of
an etymologist who tore words to pieces and
incongruously put them together again, stuffed
full of private meanings, suggestions, evocations,
absurdly, ludicrously at variance with accepted
everyday usage. As for Miss Stein, she tickled
with the incongruity of her infantile repetitious
babble and her shrewd horse-sense spiced with
Judaic irony and American humour.

Incongruity, sister to wit and to the grotesque,
is a by-road full of interest and instruction that
may ultimately lead us back enriched to the high-
road of visual as well as verbal art. It flourishes
best when, as in our day among the unhappy
few, inquiry becomes tactlessly insistent and all
values are brought to trial before a court that
believes in no law.

Caravaggio's incongruity amused the aristocratic amateurs of his day, while the young
painters were spellbound by him as only beginners
in the craft can be by the artist who enjoys the

day's success, is besieged by dealers and collectors, run after by poets and critics, admired by the aspiring masses no less than by the ladies and gentlemen of the great world. Young artists wanted to imitate his technique, his style and his more attractive subject-matter, his still-life, his concerts and most of all his card-parties.

Bellori tells us that even Guercino and Guido Reni in their early years in Rome were carried away by Caravaggio, although they soon recovered. It may be doubted whether the first ever did shake himself free, although he avoided Caravaggio's extravagances even in a work so inspired by that master as the "Jacob blessing the Sons of Joseph" (Plate 80). In Guido, on the contrary, this influence faded quickly. Yet no direct immediate follower like Saraceni and the far from negligible Gentileschi, nor any other of his Italian imitators, not even the Neapolitans Battistello Caracciolo, Massimo Stanzone, Bernardo Cavallini, Mattia Preti, have remained in the memory of men interested in the art of the past. The XVIIth-century painters who in my time were still recalled were, besides Guercino and Guido already mentioned, Domenichino, Annibale and Agostino Carracci—if indeed the last can be included. None of them, not even the two first, show much trace of Caravaggio's influence, and the greatest figure in Rome during the middle years of that century, Nicolas Poussin, betrays little acquaintance with him. He, Poussin, more than they, was an eclectic with the difference that he foraged further afield. They confined themselves to Raphael chiefly, and in a measure to Michelangelo, but he included Titian and the Carracci as well.

I am sorely tempted at this point to put in a plea for eclecticism in the visual and particularly in the figure arts. Painters and sculptors have been eclectic since the XIVth century at least. It was a question of how mobile they were, or how intelligent, or both. Thus Maso and Daddi, even if they never left Florence, looked about and found much to imitate in the Sienese Ambrogio Lorenzetti, who in turn did not wholly escape contamination by the style of Giotto. I have serious doubts about Cossa's being a pure Ferrara-Bolognese product. Too much, perhaps, has been made of his indebtedness to Piero della Francesca, but not enough to what he owed to less heroic Florentines, to Benozzo, for instance. It was not altogether wrong-headed to assign Cossa's fascinating Vatican predella (as it used to be attributed) to the Tuscan Carpaccio. And are the friezes over the arcades in Matteo di Giovanni's stupendous " Massacre of the Innocents " on the floor of the Siena cathedral conceivable without the imitation of Pollaiuolo ? There are traces of Raphael in Titian ; and would this Venetian have produced his last works without the study of Michelangelo ?

Undoubtedly the integral artists seldom wander from the broad straight way laid out by the urge of their art, its own natural growth and its own decline. Yet I am not sure that Michelangelo's youthful Pietà in St. Peter's does not betray a preference, momentary but eclectic, for Flemish types. There is in the Wallace Collection a ruined Titian based on one of Raphael's frescoes in the Pace at Rome.

Eclecticism of some sort is likely to occur the moment the artist becomes physically and mentally free to move and look about. He may go to Rome like Wagner's Tannhäuser (like Pellegrino da S. Daniele or Pordenone), and come back without having looked at anything ; he may be attracted by what is new and try to incorporate it in his own work. A Giovanni Pisano returned completely frenchified from a

journey we must infer. The mature Tintoretto
owed much to Michelangelo ; and the Cretan
Theotocupuli even more to the same Tintoretto
and to Titian, the Bassano and Veronese. But
except Theotocopuli and Giovanni Pisano, none
tried deliberately to change their nature as
artists, and even these two exceptions may have
needed the opportunity that France and Venice
gave them, to become what they were. That
was not the case with the Flemings who swarmed
to Rome to carry away grotesque graftings on
their family tree. Yet more than one of them,
Scorel for instance, had the stomach to digest
and profit by the Raphael or Michelangelo that
had fascinated and fed them.

What is eclecticism as a movement but mass-
borrowing ? If the borrowings are properly
assimilated, all is well. There, however, lurk
difficulty and danger. It takes great intelligence
and tact, and few have enough.

These few are apt to be found among the
uprooted like the two most successful eclectics
I can easily recall : Sebastiano del Piombo and
Nicolas Poussin. It is not likely that either
started out deliberately to be eclectic. The
Carraccis did, to combine the suavity of Raphael
with the power of Michelangelo and the colour

of Titian. Perhaps, if they had been as gifted
as the Venetian and Frenchman, they too might
have succeeded, and they nearly did. And a
day may come when due recognition will be
given to Burne-Jones, an artist out of time and
out of space, who had never been to Italy and
was working in the XIXth and not in the XVth
century, but used the shapes of Fra Filippo and
Mantegna to express what he and many of his
contemporaries were feeling.

What it comes to, is this : that no theorizing,
no doctrine will prevent a genius from producing
masterpieces, or help a man who is not a genius.
There has never been more serious, more exciting,
more varied talk on art and technique than in
our time. If there ever lived a painter who
knew what a picture should be, it was Charles
Ricketts. But I should be at a loss to know
where to look for his canvases now. It might
be even more difficult to discover a masterpiece
by a painter theorist greatly admired not so long
ago and still remembered, Roger Fry. On the
other hand, when real artists stoop to theorizing,
with rarest exceptions they write dull platitudes,
jejune echoes of Neo-Platonic speculations,
gathered from their learned acquaintances, but
nothing that helps to create or appreciate a specific

work of art. I have met artists in all fields :
rarely can they utter more than vague common-
places about their art. Partly because they do
not think about it and partly, no doubt, because
they have no gift for expression in words.
Leonardo seldom says anything startling, Whistler
generalizes and is more paradoxical than penetrat-
ingly suggestive.

To return to Caravaggio and his influence, it
was more beneficent out of Italy : somewhat
perhaps in France, more in Spain and at least as
much in Holland. Who not a special student
now goes out of his way to look at Velentin or
Simon Vouet ? The only Frenchmen influenced
by Caravaggio who still count are the per-
manently enjoyable Le Nain, and the now
fashionable Georges de La Tour. It is different
with Spain. Ribera, Zurbaran, scarcely would
have been what they are without him, not even
Velasquez, perhaps. The " Hilandaras " and
the " Meniñas " of the great Spaniard might not
have taken the aspect he gave them, if the
Italian's rays had not reached him : and it is
hard to believe that the " Bodegones " or the
Bacchus in his " Borrachos " were not inspired,

no matter how indirectly, by Caravaggio's way
of treating similar subjects and popularizing
them not only with painters but with the public
as well. No Italians, not even the Neapolitans,
followed Caravaggio so closely in treatment and
more still in subject-matter, in types and in
arrangements, as immediate Dutch disciples like
Honthorst (Gherardo della Notte), Hendrik Ter
Brugghen and Theodor van Baburen. There
exists no painting nearer to Caravaggio himself—
whether for lighting, for spacing or for types—
than Honthorst's " Decapitation of the Baptist "
(Plate 82) in S. Maria della Scala, in Rome.
This is only less true of Ter Brugghen's " Mocking
of Christ " (Plate 81) at Copenhagen. Other
works of this enjoyable painter are singularly
redolent of Caravaggio. So in every way,
although to a less degree, are the canvases of
van Baburen, whether in a sacred subject like
the " Entombment " (Plate 83) or in a mytho-
logical piece like the " Chaining of Prometheus "
(at Utrecht), or in concert and card-playing
pictures. All Caravaggio's Dutch followers—
and they were many—produced paintings which,
be their subject sacred or profane, are essentially
group pictures ; only they are centralized in the
Italian manner and not as in the Netherlandish

XVIth-century communal compositions so admired by Alois Riegel for refusing to be subordinated to a dominant figure, " strutting with individualistic arrogance ".

In the greatest Dutch painter of all time, Rembrandt, the influence of Caravaggio is so diffused, so spiritualized (as it were) that it is not easy to say with a few words where to look for it, or what concrete instance to cite. The case is different with Vermeer. Even his subject-matter, as in a painting like the " Toilet of Diana " at The Hague (Plate 84), suggests Caravaggio's following and far more still his chiaroscuro and preference for light that comes in from the left. Needless to observe that his chiaroscuro is as far beyond Caravaggio as, let us say, Andrea del Sarto's perspective is beyond Uccello's. It has reached the art which conceals art. You need never give it specific attention or go out of your way to admire it, whereas in their forerunners form and content were subordinated, and the chiaroscuro of the one like the perspective of the other hits you in the eye. In a sense it may be concluded that Vermeer, like Velasquez, bypassed Caravaggio, continuing and perfecting the unaggressive chiaroscuro of Belliniano in the Scuola di S. Marco, " Christ at

Emmaus ", and of Carpaccio's " St. Ursula's Dream " (Plate 23), " Reception of Ambassadors " (Plate 22) and " St. Jerome in his Study "—to speak of Italians only.

III

Enough for our purpose, these last pages on Caravaggio's effect on contemporaries as well as on early successors. What estimate my kind of student makes of him, and what appreciation, was told earlier in this essay, and I trust with sufficient clearness. I shall now attempt to speak of what German-minded authors have written and go on writing about him.

The Germans themselves, that is to say the one per cent in any nation who count, are people who remain till death at that metaphysical age which the rest of us outgrow and leave behind before puberty. When not dealing with severely quantitative matters they will " tell the clock by algebra ", as Samuel Butler charged his subtler XVIIth-century contemporaries with doing, or, as the French say, *chercher midi à quatorze heures*. Anything to avoid looking at the art object first as itself, individual and specific, as the fruit of a tree that has its own principle of growth. In fact, there will be no rational study of the visual arts (not to speak of the others) till it is assumed as axiomatic that, although it can flourish only when wind and rain are not adverse, art has its own principle of growth almost as much as any vegetable or any animal. No matter what tricks you play with grafting the seed of a carrot, it will not grow into a banana or a pear, etc. In visual arts (at least) there is an inherent principle of growth and decline, which is little influenced from outside, although its manifestations may coincide with many other contemporary manifestations in other arts, in literature, and in technical thinking. But for German-minded authors a work of art is only a springboard from which to plunge into turbid depths of the subumbilical subconscience or to rise with leaden wings into an empyrean whence they bring down theories, treatises, pseudo-histories, misinterpretations, romances, gnosticisms, occult theologies, ponderous treatises on the relation of art to the class struggle, to plagues and epidemics, to the trade in paint-brushes, to

the price of canvas, to the rent of studios, to the
kindness of hostesses, to dyspepsia, to the mother-
complex, to occupational diseases, etc. They
are given to taking periods of history which in
themselves are infinitely rich and varied and
boundless, and to packing and locking them in
with a label. The label we have to do with in
this essay is " Baroque ". What does this label,
this epithet, this term, mean ?

A person of my time, my conditioning and my
education thought it was a term used entirely
and exclusively to designate a certain kind of
visual art. Twisted columns, broken pediments,
overpowering proportions, cornices too pro-
jecting, relief too bulging, everything beyond
human expectation or demand yet with no
suggestion of the superhuman let alone the super-
natural. This much for architecture. In the
figure arts, statuesque heroic grandeur, use and
abuse, chiefly abuse of *contrapposto*—the turning
of a body on its own axis as it were—massive
limbs, swelling muscles, regal draperies, strutting
attitudes, impressive looks, all symptoms of a
forced, even tormented striving for pomp and
glory, or titanic discontent. Add violent contrasts, as in the tombs of XVIIth-century French
lay and ecclesiastical princes, potentates and

c.—G

powers, represented in full state kneeling proudly on their monuments while below we see them naked, emaciated, with worms, snakes and every other kind of vermin wriggling in and out of their gushing bowels. In verse and unexpository prose—let me say as an aside—the magniloquent, the over-elaborated, over-intricated, over-jewelled may also be called " baroque ".

So understood, all were well. But the German-minded (perhaps more numerous just now in Anglo-Saxonia than in Germany) have been applying it to the entire XVIIth century and speaking of " baroque culture ", " baroque civilization ", " baroque policies ", " baroque philosophy ", " the baroque MAN " and, in art history, of Caravaggio as the creator, initiator and completest, highest exponent of " the baroque ".

Before going further, let me say that after the baroque of Pergamon and the late Rhodian sculptures in Antiquity, the greatest, completest and most compendious master of the " baroque " that we ever have had is Michelangelo—from start to finish, from the first designs for the Tomb of Julius and their transfer to the Sistine Ceiling, to the Medici Tombs, to the Last Judgement, to the Pauline frescoes. After him, Leone Leoni, Alessandro Vittoria, the hoary Titian of the

" Martyrdom of St. Lawrence" and of his last work the unfinished Pietà, Tintoretto, but beyond all others, the most "baroque" painter who ever lived, Peter Paul Rubens.

Likewise in literature we need go no further than our own to name masters of the "baroque", each great in his way. I refer to Marlowe and Lord Brooke, to Sidney and Shakespeare in their sonnets, to Milton and Donne in prose as well as verse, to Thomas Browne, the author of *Urn Burial*, the *Garden of Cyrus* and *Religio Medici*. "Mannerists" and *concettisti* may be as sincere as others. Who will accuse Donne or to a lesser degree the sonneteers Philip Sidney and William Shakespeare of being insincere? Yet who more conceited than Donne, trying to say what had not been said before, and succeeding at times like an oil press in extracting the vivifying epithet, the illuminating, the revealing phrase. Real mannerism is the caricature style. It owes its popularity to perpetuating the same affectation and is therefore easy to recognize ; and recognition of identity is one of the most effective of mental pleasures, whether cerebral or aesthetic.

Of the music of the XVIIth century I scarcely dare speak. The little I know and understand

seems no more expressive than the visual art of
four centuries earlier. I venture to suggest that
in the XVIIth century music had not perfected
forms capable of giving utterance to what the
century in question was feeling ; for until an
art is sufficiently evolved technically it cannot
" express " its age.

To return again to Caravaggio, to my kind of
person, he would seem to be the least qualified
to serve as eponymous hero to " baroque " art
of any kind. As we have studied him, he has
turned out to be, except for his chiaroscuro and
his incongruity, almost as archaic in his concept
of the single figure as a Greek of the VIth century B.C. or a Florentine of the Quattrocento.

Why, then, are German-minded writers of
to-day so excited over Caravaggio and not over
the most compendious exponent of his age,
Rubens, or over such an exemplar of what was
most distinguished in that same period as
Velasquez ? The reason perhaps is simple
enough. Neither of those geniuses lived a disorderly life; nor after a turbid, squalid, chequered
career, died in his prime, and died sordidly.

It is the character and career of Caravaggio
that attracts to-day, and not, I venture to suggest,
his quality as an artist, and even less as a painter.

The fallacy of most men of letters, philosophers and critics, is that they will read the private life of the artist into the kind and quality of his art.

Caravaggio, according to Bellori, was fascinating in his better moments, brilliant, inspiring, attractive to highly placed amateurs as well as to the pet versifier of the day, and a " Pied Piper " to the younger painters then haunting Rome. On the other hand, he was quick-tempered and bad-tempered, intolerant, envious, jealous, spiteful, quarrelsome, a street brawler, a homicide and perhaps a homosexual. Again and again he had to run for his life from justice or private revenge. He was endowed with innumerable gifts, but with none for decent living. Except the poet Marino he kept no friends.

All this is true, but why should it have influenced his art any more than Duccio's, or Perugino's, or Cellini's ? The last two were execrable characters, homicides if not assassins ; and the first got himself taken up for drunkenness and disorderly conduct in public places. Yet what more exquisite than his paintings of the Gospel story ! What more quietistic than Perugino's compositions on wall or panel ! Cellini boasts of his prowess as a man who would not suffer affront, but I find scarcely a trace of arrogance in his so-elegant goldsmith-work, nor yet in his bronzes or marbles. If one made a business of it, one could fill books with instances of painters, sculptors, architects, musicians, whose private lives were little or no better than Caravaggio's and as little revealed in their art.

Conversely, writers keep on merrily reading into the visual products of the past, and even more of the present, all sorts of ideas, ideals, aspirations, sentiments, which were either seldom entertained, or not the least expressed. Or they generalize from what they fancy they have seen in some representation, and draw conclusions about universal states of mind at the moment when it was done.

I happened to be in Berlin three or four years after the first world war. An eminent art historian of that humiliated but impenitent German capital insisted on taking me to see a collection of paintings done in the previous few years. To my eye they were daubs imitating Parisian fashions ; and their pigment, seemingly not yet dry, suggested syrups and jams of raspberry, strawberry, greengage, plum, blackberry. I looked and a smile began to curl on my lips when my guide with tears in his eyes ejaculated : " Don't you see how the lacerated, bleeding heart of my country is expressed in these masterpieces ? " I did not.

Weeklies reach me from New York and London with articles on art exhibitions. They exalt the non-representational elegancies and decalcomanias done to-day as no great achievement of the past was exalted in its time. Sweating conviction, they write in a way so elaborate, so complicated, so subtle, that one wonders whether they as much as expect readers to follow them. Perhaps they are convinced that the less a picture, a poem, a piece of music is intelligible, the more impressive, the more absorbing, the more hypnotizing.

Compared with that kind of writing, what has been and continues to be published about the masters of other times, about " baroque " or " mannerist " artists, is reason and beauty combined. Yet it has become a scholasticism so tenacious, with such a grip, that it will take more than one Sebastian Brant, more than one Erasmus, more than one Ulrich Hutten, to laugh it back to its right place.

Few of Caravaggio's paintings that have come down to us offer grounds for characterizing him as " baroque ", let alone for considering him as the inventor or imitator or even launcher of the " baroque ". Apart from his technical innovations, he betrays nothing startlingly new, and still less revolutionary. His personal feelings seldom appear. Perhaps the Borghese " David " (Plate 55), holding a head supposed to be his own likeness, betrays a certain bitterness. If, as seems plausible, this head of Goliath was his own portrait, it may commemorate some unsavoury as well as distressing episode in his street-life, or disappointment with the great world of his patrons. There is nothing " baroque " about it, nor can I discern anything to justify the term " baroque " if we apply it to his most Quattro-cento performance, the Naples " Flagellation " (Plate 67). His " Medusa " in the Uffizi (Plate 56) is a decapitated head singularly like the reproduction that fell under my eyes the other day of a head photographed the instant after its owner was guillotined. Possibly Caravaggio was as sanguinary as the people to-day who love to witness executions. Do we say that they belong to the " baroque " age ?

For " baroque " treatment of this subject as well as of some from the Gospel story, let us turn to Rubens.

Glance at his " Medusa " (Plate 57). She is bedded in a layer of serpents, snakes, and other vermin that wriggle choreographically but do not look as if they sprang from her own head. Her mouth is not wide open but her eyes are, and stare, too expressively, over-romantically, too full of meaning. Contrast this melodramatic, truly "baroque" representation with the merely physical pain manifested in Caravaggio's " Medusa ".

Take some of Rubens' " Entombments ", the one in Berlin, another at Munich, a third at Tournai (*Klassiker der Kunst*, Plates 38, 114, 452). How frantically over-dramatized, over-expressive, compared with Caravaggio's almost matter-of-fact masterpiece now in the Vatican (Plate 48) ! Or put Rubens' " Adoration " in the Prado (Plate 86) with its splendour, its pompous bustle and its *tableau-vivant* staging, beside Caravaggio's kindred subjects at Messina and Palermo (Plates 73, 74), so impressively felt, so untheatrically presented ! Or in the Cannstadt " Sacrifice of Isaac " (*Klassiker der Kunst*, Plate 47) look at the sentimentally resigned son, the father crazed with senile grief at what is expected of him, and the graceful angel staying the wrist that was going to plunge the knife. Then glance at Caravaggio's treatment of the subject (Plate 29) as a workaday matter like the ritual slaughter of a sheep. Or again take Rubens' " Martyrdom of Peter " at Cologne (Plate 85), with its passionate melodrama, and compare it with Caravaggio's " Crucifixion of Peter " (Plate 31) reduced to a problem in lifting weights, with almost no human feeling, except, however, in the noble calm of the Saint's expression. Or yet again, take the Flemish painter-prince's " Conversion of Paul " at Munich (Plate 87), stormy, wildly agitated, all sound and fury, and contrast it with the Italian's, reduced to a *fait divers* of a frightened horse being quieted after throwing its rider.

In these scenes, and one could cite many others, compared with Rubens (whom, I repeat, I take for the supreme " baroque " painter), Caravaggio is emotionally restrained, bare, severe, more like an archaic Greek or Quattrocento Florentine. He does not attitudinize, gesticulate and " look worlds ". Far from suggesting the theatrical, he seems to avoid being as dramatic as the subject requires. Nor is he ever emphatic. Yet he can penetrate depths that Rubens never fathoms. Compare, for instance, his " Doubting Thomas " (Plate 44) with Rubens' at Antwerp (*Klassiker der Kunst*, Plate 74) or the two Peters of the last paragraph.

Conclusion : far from being inventor or foster-father of the " baroque ", Caravaggio deserves to be regarded as the most anti-baroque artist of the XVIIth century. (Parenthetically, let me add that one can trace Caravaggio's influence in all of Rubens' works just cited.)

As a better occasion may never occur, I take this one to say a few words about " mannerists " and " mannerism ", about which there is much talk and writing in German-minded circles.

The Italian word *maniera,* as used by late XVIth-as well as XVIIth- and XVIIIth-century writers, meant painting from memory, by rote, in deliberate or unconscious imitation of their most accredited predecessors—in short, what we should call " academic ". And, as a matter of fact, the most prominent practitioners of that way of doing things were founders of academies.

I am not intimate enough with German to know exactly what the word *manieriert* may mean. In French and English usage of to-day it seems to mean " affected, unnatural, forced, simpering, mincing, lackadaisical " (according to Cheval-ley's *Oxford French Dictionary*) ; while the *Oxford English Dictionary* speaks of " mannered " when

appertaining to artists as " showing mannerism ",
and defines " mannerism " as " excessive addiction
to a distinctive manner : . . . trick of style.
Hence MANNERIST."

I suspect the average use of these words to-day
combines both these attempts at definition, only
that none of the epithets in the French dictionary
should be applied to the late XVIth-century
Italian painters. Nevertheless, they are so
thought of despite the Oxford statement which
comes nearer to what I mean by " mannerist ".

I beg to be allowed to distinguish between
" manner " and " affectation ". A mannered
person, for instance, might be " affected " if he
tried to be what is usually called " natural ".
It is his nature to have unusual and exaggeratedly
individualistic ways of standing and sitting,
looking, using limbs, hands and fingers and—not
least—speech, voice, pronunciation, phrasing.
An " affected " person is one who tries to adopt
ways that are not " natural " to him—the less
natural the more reprovable.

Memory assisted by photographs and books
fails to bring up instances of late XVIth-century
mannerism comparable to those of Cosimo Tura,
Crivelli and even Botticelli—artists in some of
whose works manner almost reaches absurdity,

yet with never a touch of affectation. Of this characteristic I find much more in Sodoma, in Correggio, perhaps in Lotto, and their kind than among the " mannerists " so-called. Apart from the dry-rot which never fails to overtake academicism everywhere and always, the later Cinquecento Italians sin rather through sentimentality, I mean through the dramatization of feeling. Yet even a Baroccio does not sin that way as do Guido Reni, Carlo Dolci, Greuze and their like in later ages.

Let students take warning and stop assuming that the " mannerists " were necessarily more mannered and affected than painters of other periods. They were academic, and except that they did not produce artists so gifted they were not more academic than Guercino and Domenichino and Guido, certainly not more than Poussin and the majority of French XVIIth-century masters. And surely at no time did there exist " mannerists " (in the Italian sense of the word) more deserving the appellation than the jugglers with Raphaelesque shapes, attitudes and arrangements, like Battista Franco, Jacopino del Conte and Pirro Ligorio in their frescoes at S. Giovanni Decollato in Rome. These frescoes speak for so much enjoyment on the part of their painters, who seem to take mock war-dance attitudes and paces taught them by a great master. They were playing zestfully, delightedly and of course sincerely.

Which brings me to a point I want to make. What counts most in visual art—we are thinking of that only here—is not the manifest combination and arrangement of shapes and colours, but their power to stimulate us vitally, life-enhancingly, systemically from top to toe, not more mentally than sensuously, yet taking place in the realm of ideated sensations. *Qu'importe le flacon si le vin est bon!* True, ever so much truer than culture-snobbish, oracular art critics will admit. The trouble is that few are the inventors of new styles in flagons. In any given art there may be in a century of geniuses ten or twelve at most and in other periods fewer. Ours is already passing its first half and even Panurge has not succeeded in shaping flasks that his sheep-like imitators could use for more than two or three years. Or does he keep changing so swiftly to get away from their bleating?

To be serious for a brief moment, let me say, in other words, that the inventors of a new world of shapes, colours and composition have always been rare, but that their world, their House of

Art, could last a long time. Giovanni Pisano's and Giotto's, for instance, a full century ; van Eyck's, Masaccio's, Mantegna's, Bellini's, Correggio's, Rubens' quite a while, and Donatello's, Michelangelo's, Raphael's, Giorgione-Titian's, visibly or invisibly, till our own day.

The first tenants of these houses—to continue the metaphor—are often worthy of living in them, and occupy them to their own and everybody else's advantage. Then they sublet, and the subletters sublet, and the house falls out of repair and becomes less and less inhabitable, till it turns into a slum and finally is abandoned for a time. Generations, perhaps centuries later, for want of better housing, artists, called "archaistic", may take them up again as dwellings, and boast of their earliest occupants.

The fact is that the gifted zestful imitator of a great artist is still an artist, even if he ignores the model and " nature " and expresses himself in terms of his master. Surely that is the case with painters like Parmigianino, like Pontormo, like Rosso. And in literature do Spenser's sonnets ring less true than those of Joachim du Bellay and other versifiers of the Pléiade he translated and imitated ?

All this to dispel prejudices against the

first imitators and academicians of the right
kind.

We turn back once more to Caravaggio.
Much is made of his historical importance. We
shall not question it, although historical importance is a more subtly complicated affair than
is usually supposed. Few stop to inquire what
it "means and implies". Does it refer to any
and every event, with no thought given to its
bearing on humanity and no regard to its con-
sequences? *Cosa fatta capo ha:* what is done is
done. Or do ethical and aesthetical considera-
tions come in?

In art matters, ethical and aesthetical estimates
do count, and to the extent that an artist's works
still exist, they are alive for us and subject to our
appreciation and valuation.

In the first part of this essay I tried to say
what Caravaggio still means to a person who has
had familiar contact with the arts the whole
world has produced in the last six or seven
thousand years, and applied to him standards
that hitherto have served him to tiptoe his way
through the maze of things produced by hand.
And without reference to Caravaggio's presumed

historical importance, which is like Chaucer's Griselda " dead and buried in Itaille ".

As for Caravaggio, there remains a great deal that I cannot attempt to explain. For instance, why his types, his attitudes, his spacing, should have been so closely followed not only in Italy (in Naples especially) but in the North as well. These have little to do with his alleged innovations in the treatment of light and shade ; yet they exerted far greater influence. Vermeer, for instance, might have achieved his chiaroscuro without Caravaggio ; but without him, would he have composed a picture like the " Diana's Bath " of The Hague (Plate 84) ?

Nor can it be said that his influence in Naples even favoured what I should allow as " baroque ". It seems to have liberated bad taste enough, but few contortions and over-dramatizations. In Spain it encouraged the picaresque and in the Netherlands pictures of card-parties, concerts and convivial gatherings, but except for Rubens, Jordaens and their followers, none of their painters can be classed as " baroque ".

Historical importance is, or should be, the preoccupation of the few students whose task it is to trace sources, note replenishments, point out stagnations and refluences in the stream of events.

C.—H

In our narrow field, historically important artists are those who exerted deep influence on younger contemporaries as well as on late and remote followers, regardless of their value as artists to-day. Thus Squarcione in the second quarter of the xvth century retains historical interest because he had for direct pupils, or strongly influenced, most younger painters in north Italy, while he himself has left nothing that as a work of art rises above quaint laborious mediocrity. In Florence the dull Cosimo Rosselli had more gifted pupils and followers than Botticelli, while real creators like Piero della Francesca had, with the exception of Signorelli and perhaps Melozzo, scarcely any talented pupils and exerted an uncertain, not easily traceable influence, and that in the North rather than in Tuscany. In the Netherlands we have the more than mediocre teachers of Rubens and Rembrandt ; in Spain, Pacheco the master of Velasquez, etc., all of no artistic but considerable historical importance. Nearer to our own day, what painters, now deservedly forgotten, taught Courbet and Manet and Degas and Whistler and Cézanne, etc. ? To be a successful teacher, to exert great influence, does not necessarily require a great artist. Nor is it the wide and deep effect a Michelangelo or a

Titian has had on his art through the ages that makes either of them the creator of the master-pieces that we still live by.

I end this essay with a protest against the con-fusion resulting from the compounding, the practical identification of ethico-aesthetic values with the merely historical and the absorption of the first by the second. It has led in our time to assimilating the word " artefact " with the word " art " : any handmade rubbish, from early palaeolithic flints to the stone-scratchings on Baltic shores or Saharan wastes, the ceramics, the terra-cottas, the bronzes of pre- and proto-historic wandering tribes or of barbarian east Europeans and west-central Asiatics.

Worse still, it has led to the study of the sculpture and painting of the last few centuries for their presumed historical interest only, to the exclusion of questions of value as art. There would be little harm if it stopped there. After all, the crudest and minutest bit of sculpture or painting might point to an interesting connection, help to untwist a too-tangled coil of petty prob-lems, even provide a key to doors opening on treasures of information. But no ! The student himself is too apt to be hypnotized into exaggerat-ing the importance of his subject and to give it an aesthetic valuation, due to the zest with which his labour has rewarded him. This is immediately taken up by people interested in placing works of art that have little to recommend them except carrying an artist's name, no matter how insignificant and how recently revived.

It also leads to the search for works that are by great masters but neither representative nor worthy of their reputation. Homer nodded, and why not Titian and Leonardo or Ingres and Cézanne ! Our museums now vie with the rare private collectors in acquiring Leonardos, Castagnos, Botticellis, Peruginos, Raphaels even, that are authentic enough but calculated to give the public an incomplete or even wrong view of what they did to make them deserve the name of great masters. Private collectors may still enjoy the liberty of purchasing what their curiosity or taste or caprice demands. Museums should feel responsible to the public as educators of taste. Museums should not vie with rich amateurs in acquiring works that have little value as art but only as petty historical specimens that require no aesthetic sensibility on the part of the student who brings them to notice. They can serve only to confuse and discourage and make the thoughtful person wonder what it is all about—" why art ? "

The same merely historical interest has led increasingly in the last fifty years to exhibiting works of art in so-called historical series like postage stamps in an album or specimens in a botanical or zoological museum. It is responsible for the dismantling of such delightfully enjoyable exhibits of masterpieces only (which at the same time were monuments of taste), as the Tribuna of the Uffizi and (more deplorable still) of the Salon Carré of the Louvre. In the last-named, when a lad, like a bee hovering from flower to flower, I wandered from a van Eyck to a Leonardo and from a Leonardo to a Raphael, from a Raphael to a Holbein, from a Holbein to a Paul Veronese, from a Veronese to a Velasquez, from a Velasquez to a Poussin, etc. Now masterpieces of both Tribuna and Salon Carré have been methodically inserted in their historical series, where they are informing but pledged not to permit the formation of taste by natural growth, as muscle and brain are formed by exercise and experience.

As an example of *Historitis* that can no further go, let me cite a case that met my eye at Perugia the other day. In its art gallery there are three or four little pictures that delighted me as few others in the whole realm of painting. Almost miniatures, they could be enjoyed only on a level with the eye. Moreover, some of us think that they are by Perugino at his loveliest. They represent episodes in the legend of San Bernardino, and history seems to have proved at last that they were made along with panels by other and inferior masters to frame a banner.

So I found to my distress these exquisite works of art used as the sloping sides of a tray at the bottom of which is the just-mentioned banner (Plate 88). This banner is a painting by a local craftsman at his worst, a craftsman whose best, beside Perugino's, is rustic and childish. Yet the accessibility and the visibility of this artist's radiant works have been sacrificed to the blind muse of history. The fact that this tray stands erect and does not lie flat makes it only harder to see and to enjoy the panels plastered against its oblique sides.

I beg the reader's pardon for having seized this occasion to meander over matters I wanted to touch because they bear even if tangentially on the problem of Caravaggio as posed by certain students of to-day.

For me he is perhaps the most serious as well

as the most interesting painter that Italy produced between Tintoretto and Tiepolo. Baroque is the last epithet I should apply to him, although it is the one he now so often is graced with. Indeed, a more descriptive one would be the un-baroque or even the anti-baroque.[1]

[1] Since the above was first published, in Italian translation, there has appeared in the Atti della Accademia Nazionale dei Lincei for 1952 Lionello Venturi's *Studi radiografici sul Caravaggio* with forty-three reproductions of radiographs chiefly of the " Martyrdom of St. Matthew " at San Luigi dei Francesi in Rome (Plates 21 and 28). Plate 24 would make it plausible that in his first concept of the composition he was as classicizing as Louis David in his " Horatio and Curatii " at the Louvre (Plate 25). Nothing could be further from the " baroque ".

INDEX

Academies and academicians, 16,
17, 18, 38, 72, 75, 97, 99
Affectation in art, 98
Andrea del Sarto, 40, 65, 67, 84
Angelico, Fra, 2
Antwerp, 96

Barcelona, Santiago Alorda Col-
lection, 47 n.
Baroccio, il, 99
Baroque, the, 87 *sqq.*, 93 *sqq.*, 103,
109 n.
Bassano, Jacopo and Leandro, 26,
54, 57, 80
Battista, Franco, 99
Bellini, Giovanni, 12, 16, 26,
53 n., 54, 67, 68, 101
Belliniano, Vittore, 84
Bellori, 69 *sqq.*, 72, 77, 91
Benozzo Gozzoli, 78
Bergamo, 46, 53
Accademia Carrara, 39
San Bernardino, 53 n.
Berlin, Picture Gallery, 30, 37, 45
Bologna, Picture Gallery, 38
University, 54
Bonifazio Veronese, 12
Boston, Fine Arts Museum, 2
Botticelli, 9, 67, 98, 104, 106
Brescia, Municipal Gallery, 23
Briganti, G., ix n.
Burne-Jones, 81

Cadmus, 26
Calisto da Lodi, 54
Cambridge, Mass., Fogg Art
Museum, 12, 15
Robert Treat Paine Collec-
tion, 5
C.—H*

Campi, Giulio, 54
Cannstadt, 95
Caracciolo, Battistello, 77
Caravaggio, artistic personality of,
56 *sqq.*
character of, 55, 56, 90
critics of, 85 *sqq.*
as draughtsman, 48 *sqq.*
followers of, 13, 15, 62, 63, 76,
77, 82, 83, 84
his chiaroscuro, 8, 9, 16, 17, 18,
22, 23, 27, 29, 32, 33, 38, 40,
42, 43, 54, 57, 63 *sqq.*, 76 *sqq.*
his landscape, 10, 19, 58
his sense of space, 1, 8, 22, 32,
33, 35, 38, 42, 44, 45, 58
his treatment of religious subjects, 62, 63
his use of colour, 11, 36, 48, 59, 69
naturalism of, 53 n., 56, 71
portraits by, 40, 45 *sqq.*
predecessors of, 16, 48, 53 *sqq.*
self-portrait by, 33
Carpaccio, 16, 54, 79, 85
Carracci, Annibale and Agostino,
31, 77, 78, 80
Carritt, David, 7
Cavallini, Bernardo, 77
Cellini, Benvenuto, 91
Cervantes, 64
Cézanne, 23, 68, 104, 106
Chardin, 61
Chinese art, 2, 4 n.
Collalto, 43
Cologne, St. Peter, 96
Copenhagen, National Museum,
83
Correggio and the Correggiesque,
10, 11, 12, 14, 17, 39, 67, 99,
100

[handwritten marginal note: distribution of light & shade in a picture]

LIST OF PLATES

24 Caravaggio : X-Rays of the Martyrdom of Matthew. (*S. Luigi dei Francesi, Rome.*)

25 J. L. David : The Oath of the Horatii. (*Louvre, Paris.*)

26 Caravaggio : Matthew and the Angel. (*Picture Gallery, Berlin.*)

27 Caravaggio : Matthew and the Angel. (*S. Luigi dei Francesi, Rome.*)

28 Caravaggio : Detail of the Martyrdom of Matthew. (*S. Luigi dei Francesi, Rome.*)

29 Caravaggio : The Sacrifice of Isaac. (*Uffizi, Florence.*)

30 Caravaggio : The Conversion of Paul. (*S. Maria del Popolo, Rome.*)

31 Caravaggio : The Crucifixion of Peter. (*S. Maria del Popolo, Rome.*)

32 Caravaggio : The Conversion of Paul. (*Balbi Collection, Genoa.*)

33 Caravaggio : The Virgin and St. Anne. (*Borghese Gallery, Rome.*)

34 Caravaggio : Christ at Emmaus. (*Brera, Milan.*)

35 Moretto : Christ at Emmaus. (*Martinengo Gallery, Brescia.*)

36 Caravaggio : Christ at Emmaus. (*National Gallery, London.*)

37 Cézanne : The Card-players. (*Stephen Clarke Collection, New York.*)

38 Caravaggio : Detail of Christ at Emmaus. (*National Gallery, London.*)

39 Caravaggio : Detail of Christ at Emmaus. (*National Gallery, London.*)

40 Caravaggio (close follower of) : Christ at Emmaus. (*National Museum, Messina.*)

41 Caravaggio (close follower of) : The Doubting Thomas. (*National Museum, Messina.*)

42 Caravaggio : Concert. (*Uffizi, Florence.*)

43 Cadmus : Greenwich Village Cafeteria. (*Museum of Modern Art, New York.*)

44 Caravaggio : The Doubting Thomas. (Formerly *Neues Palais, Potsdam.*)

45 Caravaggio : Salome. (*Casita del Principe, Escorial.*)

46 Caravaggio (after) : St. Sebastian. (*Montpensier Collection, Bologna.*)

47 Caravaggio : " Madonna di Loreto ". (*S. Agostino, Rome.*)

48 Caravaggio : The Deposition. (*Vatican Picture Gallery, Rome.*)

49 P. P. Rubens : The Deposition. (*Liechtenstein Gallery, Vaduz.*)

50 Caravaggio : Eros Triumphant. (*Picture Gallery, Berlin.*)

51 Caravaggio : St. John the Baptist. (*Doria Gallery, Rome.*)

52 Caravaggio : Sleeping Eros. (*Pitti, Florence.*)

53 Caravaggio : St. John the Baptist. (*Borghese Gallery, Rome.*)

54 Caravaggio : St. John the Baptist. (*Kansas City Museum.*)

55 Caravaggio : David. (*Borghese Gallery, Rome.*)

56 Caravaggio : Head of Medusa. (*Uffizi, Florence.*)

57 P. P. Rubens : Medusa. (*Picture Gallery, Vienna.*)

58 Caravaggio (close to) : David. (*Picture Gallery, Vienna.*)

59 Caravaggio (old copy of) : David. (*Prado Museum, Madrid.*)

60 Caravaggio : Narcissus. (*Borghese Gallery, Rome.*)

61 Caravaggio : Martyrdom of Four Saints. (*S. Andrea in Vinci, Rome.*)

62 Caravaggio : St. Jerome. (*Borghese Gallery, Rome.*)

63 Caravaggio : Ecstasy of St. Francis. (*Wadsworth Atheneum, Hartford.*)

64 Caravaggio : The Death of the Virgin. (*Louvre, Paris.*)

65 Caravaggio : The Rosary Madonna. (*Picture Gallery, Vienna.*)

66 Caravaggio : The Seven Acts of Mercy. (*Monte della Misericordia, Naples.*)

67 Caravaggio : The Flagellation. (*S. Domenico Maggiore, Naples.*)

68 Caravaggio : St. Jerome. (*S. Giovanni, La Valletta.*)

69 Caravaggio : The Beheading of the Baptist. (*S. Giovanni, La Valletta.*)

70 Caravaggio : The Burial of St. Lucy. (*S. Lucia alla Marina, Syracuse.*)

71 Caravaggio : The Raising of Lazarus. (*National Museum, Messina.*)

72 Pordenone : The Raising of Lazarus. (Formerly *Collalto.*)

73 Caravaggio : Nativity. (*National Museum, Messina.*)

74 Caravaggio : Nativity. (*Oratory of San Lorenzo, Palermo.*)

75 Caravaggio : Young Woman. (*Picture Gallery, Berlin.*)

76 Caravaggio : Portrait of Olaf de Wigancourt. (*Louvre, Paris.*)

77 Caravaggio : Ecce Homo. (*National Museum, Messina.*)

78 Caravaggio(?) : Drawing of Card-sharpers. (*Lockinge House, Thomas Lloyd Collection, Wantage.*)

79 Jacopo Bassano : The Mocking of Christ. (*National Gallery of Victoria, Melbourne.*)

80 Guercino : Jacob blessing the Sons of Joseph. (*Denis Mahon Collection, London.*)

81 Ter Brugghen : The Mocking of Christ. (*Picture Gallery, Copenhagen.*)

82 Honthorst : The Beheading of the Baptist. (*S. Maria della Scala, Rome.*)

83 Van Baburen : The Deposition. (*S. Pietro in Montorio, Rome.*)

84 Vermeer : Diana's Bath. (*Mauritshuis, The Hague.*)

85 P. P. Rubens : The Martyrdom of Peter. (*St. Peter, Cologne.*)

86 P. P. Rubens : The Adoration of the Magi. (*Prado Museum, Madrid.*)

87 P. P. Rubens : The Conversion of Paul. (*Alte Pinacothek, Munich.*)

88 The Banner of San Bernardino of Siena. (*Picture Gallery, Perugia.*)

CARAVAGGIO: A BASKET OF FRUIT. MILAN, AMBROSIANA.

2

CARAVAGGIO: STILL-LIFE. NEW YORK, S. H. KRESS COLLECTION.

CARAVAGGIO: STILL-LIFE, BOSTON, MUSEUM OF FINE ARTS.

CARAVAGGIO: A FRUIT-SELLER. ROME, BORGHESE GALLERY.

CARAVAGGIO: BACCHUS. FLORENCE, UFFIZI.

6

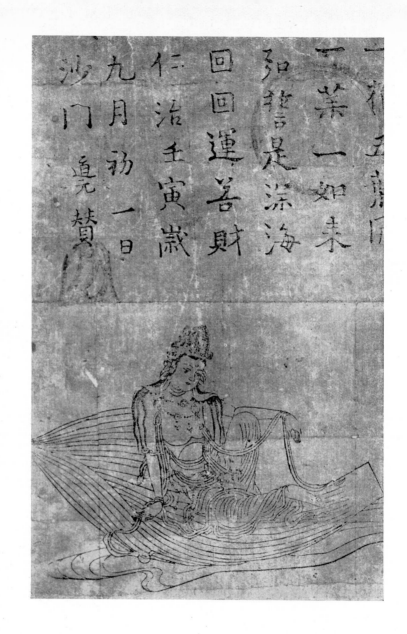

JAPANESE WOODCUT OF THE KAMAKURA PERIOD.
CAMBRIDGE, MASS., ROBERT TREAT PAINE JR.

CARAVAGGIO: BACCHUS. ROME, BORGHESE GALLERY.

CARAVAGGIO: A BOY BITTEN BY A LIZARD. LONDON, V. KORDA COLLECTION.

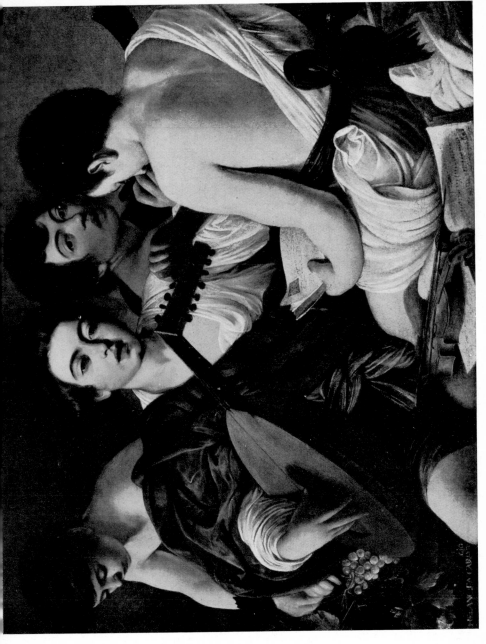

CARAVAGGIO: A CONCERT. NEW YORK, METROPOLITAN MUSEUM.

CARAVAGGIO: A LUTE PLAYER. LENINGRAD, HERMITAGE.

CARAVAGGIO: THE REST ON THE FLIGHT TO EGYPT. ROME, DORIA GALLERY.

BOTTICELLI: « LA DERELITTA ». ROME, ROSPIGLIOSI-PALLAVICINI COLLECTION.

CARAVAGGIO: MAGDALEN. ROME, DORIA GALLERY.

14

CARAVAGGIO: SOLDIER AND GIPSY. PARIS, LOUVRE.

15

CARAVAGGIO (AFTER): MARTHA AND MARY. OXFORD, CHRIST CHURCH LIBRARY.

CARAVAGGIO: THE CARD-PLAYERS. CAMBRIDGE, MASS., THE FOGG MUSEUM OF ART.

CARAVAGGIO: THE CARD-SHARPERS. FORMERLY ROME, SCIARRA COLLECTION.

18

CARAVAGGIO: SAINT CATHERINE. LUGANO, ROHONCZ COLLECTION.

CARAVAGGIO: THE CALLING OF MATTHEW (DETAIL). ROME, SAN LUIGI DEI FRANCESI.

CARAVAGGIO: THE CALLING OF MATTHEW. ROME, SAN LUIGI DEI FRANCESI.

CARAVAGGIO: THE MARTYRDOM OF MATTHEW. ROME, SAN LUIGI DEI FRANCESI.

V. CARPACCIO: RECEPTION OF AMBASSADORS. VENICE, ACADEMY.

V. CARPACCIO: SAINT URSULA'S DREAM. VENICE, ACADEMY.

24

CARAVAGGIO: X-RAYS OF THE MARTYRDOM OF MATTHEW. ROME, SAN LUIGI DEI FRANCESI.

J. L. DAVID: THE OATH OF THE HORATII. PARIS, LOUVRE.

CARAVAGGIO: SAINT MATTHEW AND THE ANGEL. BERLIN, PICTURE GALLERY.

CARAVAGGIO: SAINT MATTHEW AND THE ANGEL. ROME, SAN LUIGI DEI FRANCESI.

CARAVAGGIO: THE MARTYRDOM OF MATTHEW (DETAIL). ROME, SAN LUIGI DEI FRANCESI.

CARAVAGGIO: THE SACRIFICE OF ISAAC. FLORENCE, UFFIZI.

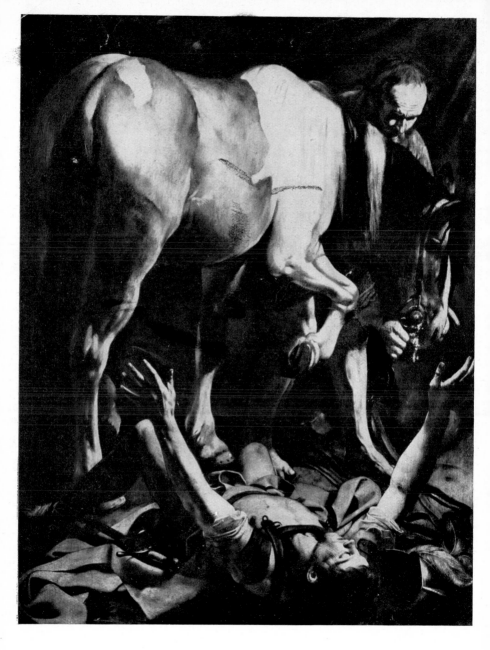

CARAVAGGIO: THE CONVERSION OF PAUL. ROME, SANTA MARIA DEL POPOLO.

CARAVAGGIO: THE CRUCIFIXION OF PETER. ROME, SANTA MARIA DEL POPOLO.

CARAVAGGIO: THE CONVERSION OF PAUL. GENOA, BALBI COLLECTION.

CARAVAGGIO: THE VIRGIN WITH SAINT ANNE. ROME, BORGHESE GALLERY.

CARAVAGGIO: CHRIST AT EMMAUS. MILAN, BRERA.

MORETTO: CHRIST AT EMMAUS. BRESCIA, MARTINENGO GALLERY.

CARAVAGGIO: CHRIST AT EMMAUS. LONDON, NATIONAL GALLERY.

CÉZANNE: THE CARD-PLAYERS. NEW YORK, STEPHEN CLARKE COLLECTION.

38

CARAVAGGIO: CHRIST AT EMMAUS (DETAIL). LONDON, NATIONAL GALLERY.

CARAVAGGIO: CHRIST AT EMMAUS (DETAIL). LONDON, NATIONAL GALLERY.

CARAVAGGIO, CLOSE FOLLOWER OF: CHRIST AT EMMAUS. MESSINA, NATIONAL MUSEUM.

41

CARAVAGGIO, CLOSE FOLLOWER OF: THE DOUBTING THOMAS. MESSINA, NATIONAL MUSEUM.

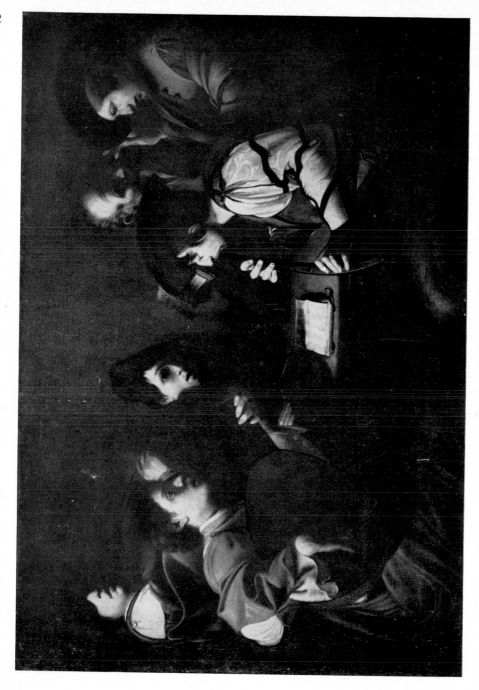

CARAVAGGIO (AFTER): A CONCERT. FLORENCE, UFFIZI.

CADMUS: GREENWICH VILLAGE CAFETERIA. NEW YORK, MUSEUM OF MODERN ART.

44

CARAVAGGIO: THE DOUBTING THOMAS. FORMERLY POTSDAM, NEUES PALAIS.

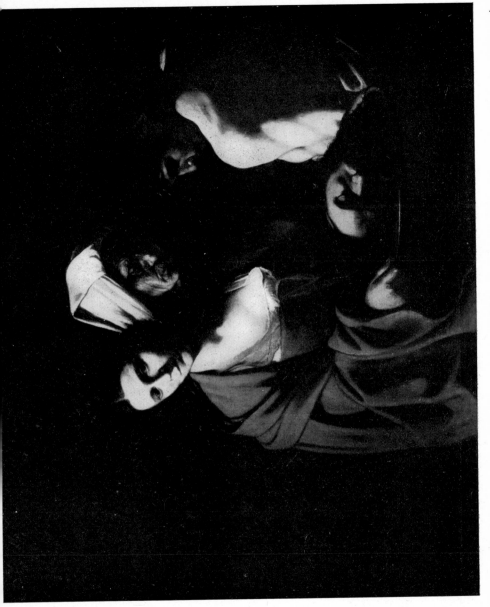

CARAVAGGIO: SALOME. ESCORIAL, CASITA DEL PRINCIPE.

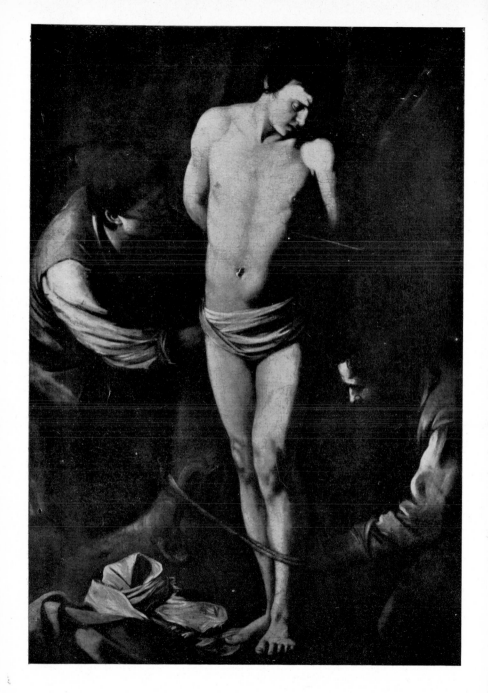

CARAVAGGIO (AFTER): SAINT SEBASTIAN. BOLOGNA, MONTPENSIER COLLECTION.

CARAVAGGIO: THE « MADONNA DI LORETO ». ROME, SANT'AGOSTINO.

CARAVAGGIO: DEPOSITION. ROME, VATICAN GALLERY.

P. P. RUBENS: DEPOSITION. VADUZ, LIECHTENSTEIN COLLECTION.

CARAVAGGIO: EROS TRIUMPHANT. BERLIN, PICTURE GALLERY.

CARAVAGGIO: SAINT JOHN THE BAPTIST. ROME, DORIA GALLERY.

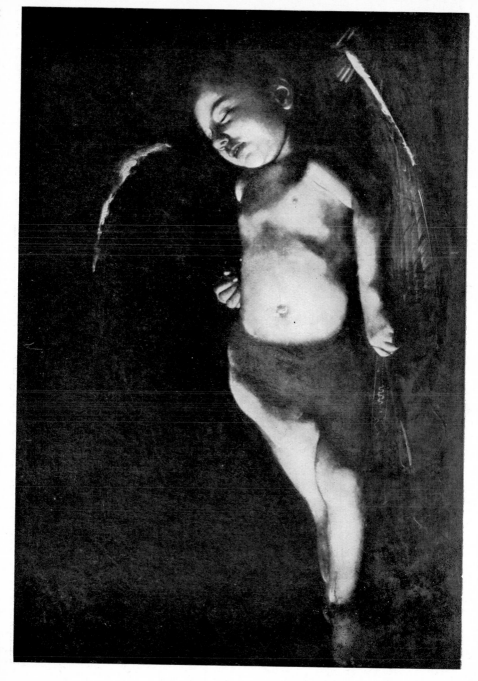

CARAVAGGIO: SLEEPING EROS. FLORENCE, PITTI PALACE.

CARAVAGGIO: SAINT JOHN THE BAPTIST. ROME, BORGHESE GALLERY.

54

CARAVAGGIO: SAINT JOHN THE BAPTIST. KANSAS CITY, MUSEUM OF ART.

CARAVAGGIO: DAVID. ROME, BORGHESE GALLERY.

CARAVAGGIO: HEAD OF MEDUSA. FLORENCE, UFFIZI.

P. P. RUBENS: MEDUSA. VIENNA, PICTURE GALLERY.

58

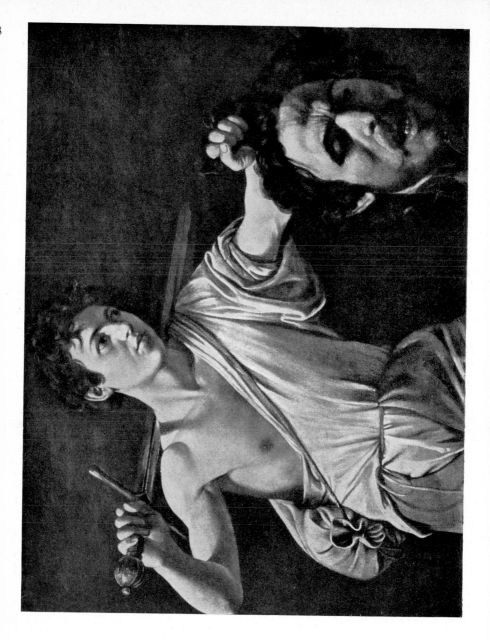

CARAVAGGIO (CLOSE TO): DAVID. VIENNA, PICTURE GALLERY.

CARAVAGGIO (AFTER): DAVID. MADRID, PRADO.

CARAVAGGIO: NARCISSUS. ROME, BORGHESE GALLERY.

CARAVAGGIO: MARTYRDOM OF FOUR SAINTS. ROME, S. ANDREA IN VINCI.

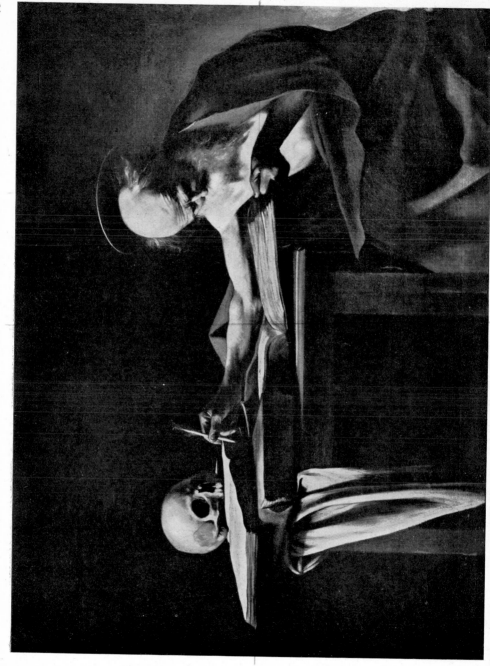

CARAVAGGIO: ST. JEROME. ROME, BORGHESE GALLERY.

62

CARAVAGGIO: ECSTASY OF ST. FRANCIS. HARTFORD, WADSWORTH ATHENEUM.

CARAVAGGIO: THE DEATH OF THE VIRGIN. PARIS, LOUVRE.

CARAVAGGIO: THE ROSARY MADONNA. VIENNA, PICTURE GALLERY.

CARAVAGGIO: THE SEVEN ACTS OF MERCY. NAPLES, MONTE DELLA MISERICORDIA.

CARAVAGGIO: THE FLAGELLATION. NAPLES, S. DOMENICO MAGGIORE.

CARAVAGGIO: ST. JEROME. LA VALLETTA, MALTA. S. GIOVANNI.

CARAVAGGIO: THE BEHEADING OF THE BAPTIST. LA VALLETTA, MALTA. S. GIOVANNI.

CARAVAGGIO: THE BURIAL OF ST. LUCY. SYRACUSE, S. LUCIA ALLA MARINA.

CARAVAGGIO: THE RAISING OF LAZARUS. MESSINA, NATIONAL MUSEUM.

72

PORDENONE: THE RAISING OF LAZARUS. (FRESCO DESTROYED) COLLALTO.

CARAVAGGIO: NATIVITY. MESSINA, NATIONAL MUSEUM.

CARAVAGGIO: NATIVITY. PALERMO, ORATORY OF SAN LORENZO.

CARAVAGGIO: YOUNG WOMAN. BERLIN, PICTURE GALLERY.

CARAVAGGIO: PORTRAIT OF OLAF DE WIGANCOURT. PARIS, LOUVRE.

CARAVAGGIO (?): ECCE HOMO. MESSINA, NATIONAL MUSEUM.

CARAVAGGIO: DRAWING FOR CARD-SHARPERS.
WANTAGE, LOCKINGE HOUSE, THOMAS LLOYD COLLECTION.

JACOPO BASSANO: THE MOCKING OF CHRIST. MELBOURNE, NATIONAL GALLERY OF VICTORIA.

GUERCINO: JACOB BLESSING THE SONS OF JOSEPH. LONDON, DENIS MAHON COLLECTION.

TER BRUGGHEN: THE MOCKING OF CHRIST. COPENHAGEN, PICTURE GALLERY.

HONTHORST: THE BEHEADING OF THE BAPTIST. ROME, S. MARIA DELLA SCALA.

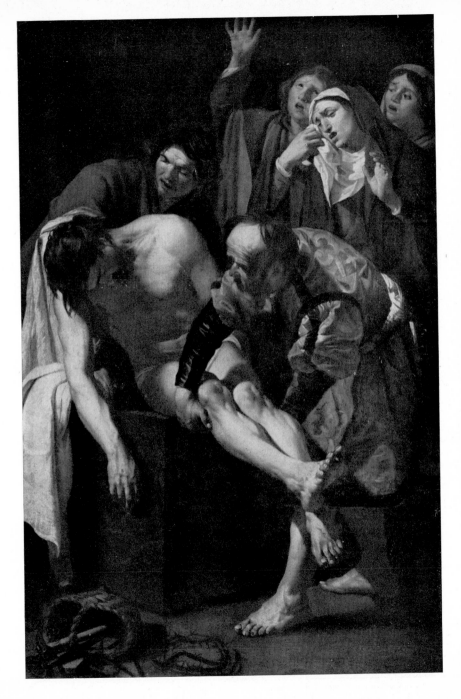

VAN BABUREN: THE DEPOSITION. ROME, S. PIETRO IN MONTORIO.

VERMEER: DIANA'S BATH. THE HAGUE, MAURITSHUIS.

P. P. RUBENS: THE MARTYRDOM OF PETER. COLOGNE, ST. PETER.

P. P. RUBENS: THE ADORATION OF THE MAGI. MADRID, RADO MUSEUM.

P. P. RUBENS: THE CONVERSION OF PAUL, MUNICH, ALTE PINAKOTHEK.

THE BANNER OF ST. BERNARDINO OF SIENA. PERUGIA, PICTURE GALLERY.